Unbroken by

PORN

Finding hope when your spouse is addicted to pornography

ASHLEY RAMOS

Dedication

This book has been and will always be for my Lord and Savior, Jesus Christ. It was His leading that led to the writing of the book, His inspiration that gave me the words to type, and His faithfulness that has sustained me.

Also, I want to take time to remember my favorite veteran, my grandfather, Elmer Glenn. It is his stories you will find spread throughout the pages of this book. His Godly example had such an impact on my life.

Special Thanks

The biggest thanks goes to my husband, Johnnie Ramos. I wouldn't have written a word of this unless he was in agreement.

Thank you to those who were my sounding board and read through chapters, listened to name ideas, and consulted with me about cover design. I greatly appreciate it!

ISBN 979-8-9877427-0-9
ISBN 979-8-9877427-1-6

UNBROKEN

1.

It Begins

May 8, 1945. Victory in Europe was declared as the Nazi's surrendered to the Allied forces. It was a day of rejoicing, and a day where many people were finally able to exhale and breathe easily at the thought of their GI Joe coming home. April 10, just 28 days before, the only sounds in the town of Laudenbach, Germany were those of gunshots. Not just one or two shots, but it was a firefight. One US soldier was lying in the street, clinging to life. And his fellow soldiers were shooting toward the snipers as fast as their guns would allow. Finally, the last shot was fired and the sniper, along with the soldier in the street, was dead.

This day in April was one of the toughest experiences that Elmer Glenn faced battling the Germans in WWII. He and his fellow men in the 4th Infantry Division had marched from

Utah Beach, France to central Germany battling the German powers. Along the way, they had 199 days of consistent contact with the enemy. Mr. Glenn tried to forget that day in April, but he could never put it behind him. See, it was he, along with some other men, that returned fire from a building the day their fellow soldier, Graham, was shot and killed in the streets. And it was him that fired the shot that silenced the sniper once and for all.

Graham wasn't just a fellow soldier, but he was Glenn's foxhole buddy. They had grown to be like brothers over the six months they were fighting together. And Graham, he had a lot to live for. He, like Glenn, was a young man. Graham was married in 1943. Shortly before he left for the war, his wife had gotten pregnant, but Graham was shipped out before his child was born. He was just 28 days away from getting to see his son.

Unfortunately that day in April 1945, Graham made a mistake. In the words of Glenn, "Graham did something stupid. He shouldn't have been walking out in the street like that." Immediately after the shots rang out that killed Graham, Glenn and another soldier started shooting from the window they were in toward the area the initial gunfire came from. They kept shooting and shooting until Glenn killed the German soldier that killed Graham. When the firefight was over, the wood on their gunstocks was smoking from all the ammunition they shot. As they looked around them, they noticed the area all around the window was riddled with bullet holes, but none had ever hit them.

This soldier, Elmer Glenn, is my grandfather. Growing up I always heard the story of the day he lost his closest friend, Beverly Graham. Glenn, Pap as I call him, said he always felt bad because he didn't know Graham's address. They had grown to be like brothers, and he didn't even have a way to contact his family after the war was over. Luckily, technology advanced and one of my cousins was able to track down Graham's family in the early 2000s. Pap was finally able to go visit them and tell them what he had been waiting over 60 years to tell them—that he was with Graham the day that he died. Pap got to meet Graham's wife, the son Graham never met, and was also able to see where Graham was buried.

Graham's story never gets old. It may sound shocking, but when it comes to porn, it's an extremely easy story to relate to. See, my husband, much like Graham, did something stupid. He was young and made a decision that affected the rest of his life. The decision he made, the enemy capitalized on, and the bullets of addiction lodged deep within him.

As his wife, I had a choice. Am I going to let him die in the street? Am I going to just say, "You did this to yourself. Now you have to pay." Or am I going to grab my gun, and fire and keep attacking until the advances against my best friend have ended? Johnnie's physical life was never in danger like Graham's, but our marriage was. Our family was. You have the choice to call it quits and step away.

Or you can fight. You can refuse to give up, even though you are taking on enemy fire. Even though you are standing in a bullet-ridden building, you can still have the victory. Symbolically, you may be wounded. Your spouse may be bleeding out, in desperate need of help, and you have a decision to make. You can hide behind a wall and hope to stay safe. Or you can fight. This book is for the fighters. This book is for the women who say I am not going to attack my spouse who is wounded, but rather I'm going to fight the real enemy. Could I be hurt in the process? You bet. But you also have the chance to take out this addiction once and for all.

You'll hear more about my grandfather and his stories from the war. There are some stunning parallels to how we, the wives, can move forward despite grievous mistakes made. It is a process. But we're going to talk about the steps to take to move past some of the hurt and move toward reconciliation and lasting change.

A pornography addiction is a very personal situation to discuss; not just for the person addicted, but for the spouse too. Many don't want to talk about it because nobody is that honest, right? I mean think about it. We live in a world where everything is edited or only the best picture of the twenty you took is posted. We have the acting game down. Nobody is honest enough to put everything on the line and bear their soul with their spouse. But my husband was. He had a moment of honesty where he confessed what he had been doing. And from that time in our marriage, over the years, he has had honest and open conversations about what is going on in his head.

Has he told me everything? Of course not. Do I want to know all the details? Of course not. But instead of hiding in the darkness, he chose to bring his shortcomings to light. But no one is that honest, are they? If you start to talk about porn or lust in any type of mixed company, you have the guys who are playing the acting game trying not to fidget or act like they are the ones who have succumbed to temptation. The women are thinking, "Oh, of course it isn't my husband who is dealing with that, it's probably Sally's husband." Statistically speaking, it isn't just Sally's husband. It could very easily be all our husbands.

My spouse confessed his addiction to me before I found the evidence. I know that is not everyone's story, and I also know that sometimes you find out about your husband's porn addiction by chance, not by honesty. He looked at porn, got hooked, and now you're hurt. One big, bold moment of honesty has changed our marriage, and hopefully the honesty that we have had in our marriage can help restore yours. Now, we are choosing to have that moment of honesty with you. Is it easy to talk about what we've been through over the years? No, in fact, it's incredibly awkward!

Before we really get started, I want to make a couple of statements. First, this was written with the full permission of my husband. He is in a much different place now than where he was at the height of his addiction. When I approached him about this idea, he told me that while it is uncomfortable and even embarrassing talking about his porn addiction, if what he went through personally and what we went through as a couple can help someone, then it is worth it.

Secondly, let's agree not to think any less of anyone mentioned here. We all have things we have dealt with, are dealing with, and will deal with one day. I love my husband more than he will ever know and I hope that no one will think less of him because of the struggles he has had. That said, let's begin.

For most of my life, I was fairly sheltered. I was innocent about a lot of sexual things for much longer than a lot of people, but I'm glad I was. After spending my elementary school years at a Christian school, I started middle school in a public school, and I was quickly educated in that area! I realized there were very few people who had any desire to be sexually pure. It was about this time I learned what pornography was. I didn't watch it or have anything to do with it, I just knew it existed. I figured it existed far away from me and it wasn't something people I knew dealt with.

In college, my naivety came to end. I was rocked by

staggering statistics of the students in my church who dealt with porn. My best friend, who later would be my husband, was another example of someone who was exposed early in life and was hooked for many years. It was during this time I realized that porn was everywhere. It had been all around me this whole time, affecting generations of people, but no one was talking about it. Speaking of that, let me tell you about Peru and the time I almost embarrassed myself.

It was around this time in college, I went on a missions trip to Lima, Peru. Our flight arrived in the middle of the night, and as one of the leaders of the trip, it was important for me to stay awake. By this time, I was mentally and physically exhausted. We were driving through the streets of Lima and as I looked out the window of the bus, I saw business signs advertising for brothels, or so I thought I did. I couldn't believe my eyes. Throughout the city, business after business. I was about to say something about my disgust for their sexual perversion. Not only did they have numerous brothels in the city, but they were lit up in bright neon signs! At least people in the States tried to hide their sexual addictions, but here, there was no shame! What was I getting myself into?

However, just as I was about to say something, I realized in my exhaustion, I had confused the word "brothel" and "hostel". Lima did not have big signs all over the city advertising brothels, but rather hostels. Needless to say, I was so glad I didn't embarrass myself and say something stupid about perceived sin.

That night, I thought their sexual perversion was so obvious. But, I was wrong. There are times when problems and addictions may be obvious, but many times, you may not know someone is dealing with a sexual addiction—even your spouse.

I know I was surprised, and you may have been shocked when you found out what your spouse was dealing with, too. For many, a porn addiction is an issue in their marriage and it is up to them to decide if they want to do the hard work and see their marriage restored.

Thankfully, there are a lot of resources focused on the person who is addicted. However, most don't realize the desperation that is on the spousal side of a sexual addiction. What does the wife say to her husband when she finds his stash? How do you deal with sexual failure when you are not the one who has failed, but it has been your partner? A pornography addiction is an important topic, and it isn't to be taken lightly. How you react can play an instrumental role in your spouse finding freedom from this issue.

So, let's dive in and take this head-on. No doubt, you are reading this because someone you love has had a problem with pornography, and you don't know what to do about it. If you are anything like me, you have gone through the emotions of feeling betrayed, upset, and saddened by the actions taken. You may have walked down the path of self-blame and are carrying the weight of this compromise (and probably repeat compromise) on your shoulders.

I don't know your story, but I know mine. While the details of each story are different, some of the emotions are the same. It's easy to think that my hurt is worse than yours because of the specifics of each circumstance, but at the root of it all, we are each dealing with betrayed trust and misplaced intimacy. I'm going to continue to tell you a small portion of my story. Some of the insights I share will be pivotal in further concepts, so I wanted you to know the whole story at the beginning.

As I previously mentioned, I was sheltered until public

school, where my naive world came crashing down. I'm glad I was sheltered for as long as I was, but there comes a time when you need to stop being ignorant of the issues that surround you and do something about them. I was saved at the age of 9, and I've always taken my relationship with the Lord very seriously. During my teenage years, I was kind of an oddball. I tried to fit in, but my commitment to God came first, which meant I didn't do things that a lot of other kids my age were doing. I didn't dress like most of them, and I didn't act the same way or use the same type of language that many of them did, so it was hard to make friends when I started attending a public school.

From a combination of things, I had low self-esteem. I didn't think I was pretty. What didn't help was that all my friends had boyfriends and I had no offers. That just reinforced the feelings I had inside. Of course, middle school can be rough, and it was rough for me. High school was a little better, but I still had no offers to go on a date and felt out of place. In ninth grade, I had a girl tell me that I must be a lesbian since I hadn't had a boyfriend. I knew that wasn't the case, but it was hurtful.

In retrospect, I am glad I didn't date in high school. However, I also wished I better understood where to find my value. During high school, I felt God was calling me to be a missionary and I told Him I would go wherever he led me. Because of that call, I started going on mission trips and it was during one of those trips that I finally started taking steps toward being free from some of the self-esteem problems I was having. I finished high school, still single, but having a much better view of myself. Despite the things that were said in jest or jokes played on me because I was single, I knew God had a plan.

I attended Lee University in Cleveland, TN, with initial

plans to become a missionary. On the first day of my freshman year in Dr. Doolittle's class, I met the man that was going to change my life forever, the man who would later be my husband: Johnnie Ramos. There is a long story of how we started dating and became engaged and it is a wonderful, funny story. However, it isn't the point I'm trying to make. We met my freshman year and became close friends as the year progressed. By November of my junior year and after much prayer, Johnnie felt like God had told him that I was the one he was supposed to marry. We finally started dating and 19 months later we were married.

At some point before we were dating, Johnnie told me about his problem with porn. While I didn't like the fact that he had struggled with that addiction, my naivety bubble had already burst. I knew it was common for most guys to have seen porn. I had never had sex or even seen a man naked. Nothing. I valued my purity, and it was hard thinking that something I valued didn't seem to have as much value to the rest of my generation. Nonetheless, I told him I didn't hold it against him. We talked about it occasionally as I had questions that I couldn't wrap my mind around. He graciously tried to answer them.

For him, this was not a new issue. Johnnie was shown his first magazine by some kids in his neighborhood when he was around nine years old. That's right, nine years old. As much as I would like to say that is an early age, statistics show otherwise. Since the age of nine, Johnnie has had these inappropriate images in his head. As he progressed through middle school and high school, things only grew worse. As children of the late 80s, the internet became popular for us during the late 90s and early 2000s, which made porn much easier to come by. For Johnnie, he usually used his home computer. Because of the lack of information about this issue during that time, his computer was left unchecked. In talking with my in-laws, they look back and can't believe they didn't realize what was going on.

After graduating high school, Johnnie spent the summer in Bolivia with his parents who, at the time, were serving as missionaries to that particular country. Toward the end of the summer and before Johnnie started college at Lee, he attended a youth camp in which his father was preaching. Since they were in Bolivia, his father was preaching in Spanish. While Johnnie had grown accustomed to hearing Spanish, he wasn't fluent. Toward the end of his father's sermon, his father made a statement in Spanish that Johnnie actually heard in English. He said, "Today, your life is changed." And it was. That night Johnnie encountered God's presence unlike he ever had before. Pornography didn't have the same grip on him that it once did. He was changed. Porn was still something he struggled with from time to time, but by the time we were getting married, I thought it was a non-issue. However, I was very wrong.

I don't remember the day Johnnie told me he had been looking at porn again. While most remember the day and time their children were born or when they got married, this was different. This was a day I wanted to forget. We had been married less than six months and as we were walking to our cars after an evening church service he told me he had been looking again. I was devastated. You know what, I don't think "devastated" really conveys the emotions I was feeling. I was crushed, torn apart, and upset. Luckily, we had driven separately that night because I don't know what it would've been like riding back home with him. I took the entire forty-minute drive home crying from the depths of me. I know that sounds dramatic, but I was in some serious pain.

As you can probably remember from a few pages previous, I had some major self-esteem issues I had to work through toward the end of high school and into college. While I had a much better view of myself, it was still my weak area. Unfortunately, I didn't know how to guard my mind or take my thoughts captive, as Paul mentions in 2 Corinthians 10:5. Anyway, I cried and cried. I was also wondering how I was going to face him when I got home. Nothing had prepared me for this moment. I had no idea how to respond when my husband—my one and only—told me he was looking at porn. Not much was said for a while that night, but I felt like God was telling me, "Forgive him. Forgive him, now."

JOHNNIE: I thought I'd be okay. I thought I could handle the addiction on my own. But I couldn't.

Forgive him...
Forgive him, now.

2.

Forgiveness

orgive him? Without question, I did immediately. Honestly, in that moment I'm not sure if I told him that I forgave him, or if I just started treating him like I had forgiven him. But I know I eventually told him that I forgave him. I can't explain the feelings I felt when I made the choice to forgive him. While I was obviously hurting, there was also a sense of peace that came over me. You should be aware that there are times when your mindset and words don't match. You may say, "I forgive you." Then proceed to treat whomever as if they are not forgiven. Conversely, you may not utter the words, "I forgive you." But you act as if the offender is forgiven. Both need to happen. You need to forgive with your words and with your actions. When you choose to forgive, you are choosing to no longer hold the offense against the offender. In this case, you can choose not to hold your husband's porn addiction against him. Forgiveness doesn't mean you aren't sad, and it doesn't mean that there won't be consequences for the offense, but rather you are choosing not to hold this indiscretion against your spouse.

You may say to yourself, "There is no way I can forgive him." And I've been there. Those were my initial thoughts. It was hard because I wanted to be his first and only, but I wasn't. There were images that came before me, images that looked better than me, and images that seemed flawless compared to what I saw in the mirror. It wasn't just a choice he made before we were together, it was a choice he made after we were married. It wasn't accidental, it was purposeful. I didn't want to forgive him. I wanted to hold onto my hurt and dwell on it. I felt I was entitled to that and all the emotions—the sadness, hurt, anger,—I could hang on to them because he hurt me so badly. Holding on to those feelings gave me a sense of control and in circumstances like that, feeling like I had some control gave me a false sense of security. The reaction I had, and perhaps it is the same one you are having, is common and even expected! But just because it is common, it doesn't mean it is the right reaction to have.

JOHNNIE: Note to women: It's not just the physical attributes. For guys, it starts that way because you are seeing naked women. But then, it becomes about control. You can choose when and how you want it.

I can't say I was ready to forgive Johnnie, rather it was out of obedience to the Word of God. You might be saying the same thing, "But I'm not ready to forgive." Or maybe you just don't want to let it go. Ask yourself why. Maybe your spouse didn't apologize or maybe this keeps happening. Either way, you are hurt, so your reaction is to withhold forgiveness. When you withhold forgiveness, it gives the illusion that you are controlling the situation. While control feels good when it feels like the circumstance can't be controlled, it still is not how it should be handled. This isn't a control fight. This is a restoring your marriage and restoring your heart fight.

This isn't the time to hold a grudge or have the mindset of, "He hurt me, so I'm going to stay mad. I don't have to be nice. In fact, I'm going to use this to hurt him." I know you may not have those exact thoughts, but it's easy for thoughts to tend toward that direction. If you keep following a mindset like that, you are going to fall into a self-perpetuating cycle of hurt and more hurt.

When Christ tells us to forgive, He tells us to forgive no matter the circumstance, over and over again. It applies to everyone, no matter how deep the hurt. Matthew 18:21-22 AMP says, "Then Peter came to him and asked, "Lord, how many times will my brother sin against me and I forgive him and let it go? Up to seven times?" Jesus answered him, "I say to you, not up to seven times, but seventy times seven." Those verses are sobering because it tells us that we need to continue to forgive even if the offense is repeated. I don't know your story, but in my story, Johnnie's confessions were repeated again and again. Yes, you have an opportunity to hold this compromise—and possible repeat compromises—against your spouse, but, as one pastor pointed out, it's also an opportunity to forgive.

Forgiveness can be hard, but have you ever thought about why? Why is it so hard to forgive someone when they have hurt you so badly? It seems as if the bigger the infraction, the harder it becomes. Unfortunately, no matter how big or small the offense, our ability to forgive boils down to a sense of pride. Let's take a look. We don't want to get hurt. Just to be clear, I am not talking about physical violence and your safety, I'm speaking only to forgiveness from emotional hurt, and more specifically the forgiveness between a husband and a wife. When we get hurt, we tend to put up walls as defenses to keep from getting hurt again. Makes sense, right? Who wants to get hurt again, anyway? Well, let's see how this plays out.

Pride comes in two different ways. First, pride says, if I control the circumstance, I can better control if I get hurt again. Yes, I'm sure you know the Bible says to forgive, but not forgiving and keeping your spouse at an arm's distance seems safer. Forgiving seems counter-intuitive, because if I forgive, I am opening myself up and choosing not to hold the offense against my spouse. What if he thinks he is off the hook? What if he takes advantage of my forgiveness and keeps repeating these actions? He may keep hurting me. This shows a big flaw in our nature. Control is our way; forgiveness is God's way. When we choose to operate in our own power and do what we think will work instead of God's plan, that is simply pride.

A second way pride can come in is in the area of revenge. Once we forgive, we are forfeiting our right to "get back" at our spouse for the pain they inflicted on us. Some may think it is unbelievable that there are people who want to "get back" at their spouse, but it's not unbelievable. Many seek payback because they want their spouse to know that they haven't bested them, and they intend for their spouse to feel some emotional pain, too. However, Romans 12:17 AMP says, "Never repay anyone evil for evil. Take thought for what is right and gracious and proper in the sight of everyone." Revenge is never appropriate and while it may feel good at the time, it is choosing the low road, instead of the road of God's plan. It is time to put pride aside and choose the path of forgiveness.

Forgiveness can be tough. It sure wasn't easy for me. So, if you are having a hard time making the decision to not hold your husband's addiction against him, I understand, and Jesus does too. While humans fail in this area, we can be grateful there is a perfect example to look to in Jesus. Not only did he forgive those who put him to death, but he died for the forgiveness of all of humanity for all of time. It wasn't just our spouse's addiction that nailed Jesus to the cross, but it was our sins as well. He forgave us so we could be in relationship with Him. Not because we are inherently good, not because we could do anything for Him, but just because He loves us and wants to be in an eternal relationship with us.

Don't misunderstand Jesus' time on Earth. He was fully God, but He was also fully human. In Hebrews 4:15 AMP the Bible says, "For we do not have a High Priest who is unable to sympathize and understand our weaknesses and temptations, but One who has been tempted [knowing exactly how it feels to be human] in every respect as we are, yet without [committing any] sin." This verse says nothing about it being easy to forgive or that it was easy for Jesus to go through life without sinning. It implies the opposite. It says that He knows what it is like.

I know some people would say this verse means we should just forgive our husbands and get over it. As if to say that Jesus is in Heaven responding to us scoffing, "Really? You're having trouble forgiving your husband for looking at porn? Come on, people killed me, and I forgave them. I don't see what your problem is." However, that is not the case. Yes, He was tempted like we are and yes, He did not sin. But because He was fully man, He understands our pain. Of all people, He is the one who could say, "I did it, so can you. Let me help you." With that verse as an example, you can see the first step in repairing your marriage and healing your hurt is choosing to forgive your spouse.

In trying to better understand forgiveness, we are going to look at two questions:

1. Why should I forgive?
2. How can I forgive when the hurt is deep?

Knowing the "why" is a key motivation for any action. Why should you do your dishes? So, you don't get bugs. Why should you fill your car up with fuel? If you don't, you won't be going anywhere! Having a 'why' is a powerful motivator. It takes people from inaction to action because they have a purpose for their actions. From day-to-day decisions to starting your own business, you need to know your "why"! So, let's answer the 'why' regarding forgiveness. Why forgive as a first step?

A powerful first motivator is that you can't be healed and whole unless you forgive. You can't have reconciliation in your marriage until you forgive. As I'm sure you may know, the Bible tells us to forgive. In Mark 11:25 AMP the Bible says, "Whenever you stand praying, if you have anything against anyone, forgive him [drop the issue, let it go], so that your Father who is in heaven will also forgive you your transgressions and wrongdoings [against Him and others]." This is not the only verse that commands us to forgive and even hinges our forgiveness on our ability to forgive others when they wrong us. Unforgiveness is a bacteria the enemy, Satan, can feed off. He will turn that unforgiveness into bitterness and eventually hatred. In Hebrews 12:14-15 ESV, it says, "Strive for peace with everyone, and for the holiness without which no one will see the Lord. See to it that no one fails to obtain the grace of God; that no "root of bitterness" springs up and causes trouble, and by it many become defiled".

The author of Hebrews references a "root of bitterness". Let's talk about roots. I am not vigilant about pulling weeds from my yard. I see them when I walk in the house and think that I should get out there and take care of them, but it rarely happens. Despite my lack of vigilance, I do know there are three ways to pull weeds. My son's way, my way, and my dog's way. When my son was 3 and was helping me pull weeds, he would just pull the leaves off the weeds, which does nothing long term. It makes the area look better because you don't see the proliferation of leaves everywhere, but the roots are still there. He was 3, and he didn't know any better. He didn't understand that unless you get the root, the weed is still there. Still, he proudly pulled those leaves right off and tossed them in the trash can, convinced he had fixed the problem and did a job well done!

Then there is my way, I know I must get the root. So, I usually get the root. The little ones are easy, but some of the bigger weeds are tough! They are tough to grab with gloves on, but at the same time, I don't always want to get my hands dirty and pull them up bare-handed. Inevitably, some of the big ones tend to stay right there and they continue to grow unrestrained until my son comes and pulls all their leaves off.

Lastly, there is my dog's way. Toby obliterates weeds. I will point to a weed and tell Toby to get the weed and he will dig and dig until the weed is gone. It's not just gone, but the conditions aren't even susceptible for the weed to re-grow because there is a big hole! There is nothing left. After he digs for a few moments, he then sticks his black, wet nose to the ground and begins to inhale. He draws long sniffs of the dirt. Depending on what he smells, he may keep digging until he is satisfied that the area is clear.

We are the same way in our treatment of bitterness and unforgiveness. Some of us do the equivalent of what my 3-year-old did. We do what we can to make things look better. We don't want people to think we are having marriage problems, or perhaps we don't want our kids to think something is wrong. So, we get rid of the obvious, visible evidence of our bitterness, but we aren't actually taking the root out, we still haven't forgiven. We're putting on a front. We can even convince ourselves that things are better, just as my son proudly trots away after pulling the leaves off. Oh, it looks better, so things must be improving! But, because we haven't dealt with everything under the surface, the issue remains. It's only a matter of time before the same feelings come back. In fact, they may even spread to different areas of your life.

Ultimately, you know you need to get to the root of the issue and fully forgive your spouse. You can do activities or actions that are only for show, but you know you must genuinely take care of the root of the issue. You KNOW this, but it doesn't always produce actions. You do your best. You try. You realize that you need to genuinely forgive, but when it gets hard, you don't always fight through it.

It's easy to forgive when someone takes your parking spot. It's a little tougher when someone says something rude about you. But you can usually handle it, and forgive that person. But something like a porn addiction is tough, it's way past stolen parking spots and snide comments, this is a deeply personal hurt from the person you trust the most. Forgiveness for your husband requires hard work to get that root out. It's something you must keep working at. Instead of getting in there and getting your hands dirty, it's easy to go halfway. Emotionally, you try and ignore it and never deal with it until the issue creeps back up. If you do this long enough, it is no better than how my son handled weeds. The weed is still there because the root is there.

Lastly, you have Toby's way. I want to treat all unholy roots in my life as Toby treats them in my yard, with laser focus and determined intensity. He doesn't stop because he's dirty, he doesn't stop because it is hard. He doesn't stop until the job is done, and he triumphantly trots away with dirt clumped under his claws and a dirt-stained nose. Do we forgive like that? Do we eradicate all bitterness from our lives like that? I hope we do because that is the only way to truly get rid of the bitterness and unforgiveness that is keeping us from moving on and experiencing healing.

Something else about Toby's method is that it leaves the area inept to produce more weeds. Ephesians 4:26-27 ESV says, "Be angry and do not sin; do not let the sun go down on your anger, and give no opportunity to the devil." One thing I love about this verse is that it validates emotions. It clearly states that you can be angry and not sin. In having personal experience with a spousal porn addiction, I don't see how a person could hear this news from their husband and not be angry!

The second portion of the verse contains an interesting mandate—don't let the sun go down on your anger, so you don't give the devil an opportunity. Some versions call it a foothold. It is telling us to not even fall asleep before we "clear the air" so to speak. Just as Toby will literally dig a hole to ensure the weed is gone and that it can't grow back, we must clear the air and forgive our spouse so bitterness and unforgiveness have no place to grow.

Notice, the verse didn't say, "Don't go to bed sad." I'm not suggesting that you must completely recover from the shock and pain of the news all before bedtime. I am suggesting, and the Bible is mandating, that you must not go to bed angry. Forgive your spouse before you go to sleep, forgive him immediately, forgive him completely. Don't hold it from him. Make the choice that you are not going to hold on to the offense. Remember, forgiveness doesn't mean that you condone the behavior, it just means that you are choosing not to hold the offense against the person. However, it also doesn't mean that you simply forget about it, either. You must act wisely going forward to not hold the infraction against your spouse, but to also make decisions that will help bring recovery.

At the end of the verse, it says to do this so the devil will not have an opportunity or have a foothold. Have you ever wondered where the foothold is? Is it in you or in the offender? I think that it is speaking about you. Meaning, even though you may not have done anything wrong, because you don't forgive your spouse it can give the devil an opportunity to have a foothold in your life. It's like a two-for-one deal for the enemy! He is not only entangling your husband in a porn struggle, but he is also entangling you because you are angry and not forgiving. Choosing to forgive your spouse is that important.

A final reason why we should forgive is for the person who needs forgiveness. As John and Lisa Bevere said in a podcast,[1] forgiving the offender is giving them a vote of confidence. It communicates that you believe in them! When you have a spouse that is struggling with porn, they need a vote of confidence.

One of the hardest perspectives to overcome as a wife in this battle is the perspective of being the victim. It seems very logical, and in some measure it is true. But to see lasting change in you both, you must remember that this is going to take effort and understanding from both of you. I know for Johnnie, he already felt hopeless by the time he told me about his addiction. If I were to regurgitate those same feelings back to him, nothing would change. But when we worked together—him knowing my hurt and me knowing his desperation, then things began to change. However, it all started with forgiveness and me giving him the vote of confidence and knowing that I wasn't going to hold this offense against him.

Notes:

1. Bevere, John & Lisa. "Special Valentine's Day Episode: Marriage Makeover." Conversations with John and Lisa Bevere." 24 February 2017. https://messengerpodcasts. com/special-valentines-day-episode-marriage-makeover/

3.

How to Forgive

Now that we have discussed the importance of why you should forgive, let's talk about the practical step of "how to forgive." It's easy to forgive someone when the offense isn't that big. But when you need to forgive someone who you don't want to forgive—you may even feel you can't forgive—it becomes a struggle. Are you ready for the complex process of forgiveness? Here it is: make a decision and do it. That's it. How do you forgive someone? You decide in your heart that you are not going to hold the offense against them and then you stick by your decision.

It's worth repeating from the last chapter, forgiveness doesn't mean you aren't sad, and it doesn't mean that there won't be consequences for the offense, but rather you are choosing not to hold this indiscretion against your spouse. But, this also means that you have to let it go, so no bringing up their struggle in an unrelated argument to try to win the fight.

I'm sure I'm not the only one who has done that. Just remember, forgiveness is the will of God. God never wants you to live in unforgiveness. When you are praying about this situation, ask God to help you forgive. Because we know it is the will of God for us to forgive, we can be confident that He will answer that prayer and help. But the bottom line is to make the decision, then to let it go.

I know it may sound crazy but hear me out on this one. Your feelings aren't always going to agree with the decision your mind makes. You won't always feel like forgiving your spouse. You will have those thoughts creep in that will try to convince you to slip back into unforgiveness. A verse that was referenced earlier, 2 Corinthians 10:5 AMP says, "We are destroying sophisticated arguments and every exalted and proud thing that sets itself up against the [true] knowledge of God, and we are taking every thought and purpose captive to the obedience of Christ". This verse applies not only to the topic at hand but has many applications. Honestly, this verse is great to keep in mind for the one who is struggling with the porn addiction, too. We are encouraged in this verse to capture every thought and make it obedient to Christ. So, whatever thoughts we have that do not line up with Christ's standards, we are to capture them, release them, and replace them with the truth of God's word.

How does this work, exactly? Let me take you through a scenario. Your husband tells you he was looking at pornography again. You are frustrated and sad, as this was the second time this week—and it's only Wednesday. You make the choice to forgive because you know God tells us to forgive. Later that evening, you are doing dishes and thinking about what happened during the day. Suddenly, you are reminded of the conversation you had, and all those emotions come flooding back. You are upset, and you have those thoughts of, "I'm not letting him off the hook that easy. No, I don't want to let it go. It doesn't matter if I hold onto it a little longer. He really isn't sorry since he did it again, so he doesn't deserve it. At this point, I don't know if our marriage will last anyway." And your mind keeps going down this track—stop it right there.

You can't control what happens in the future, but you do control your outlook and how you choose to respond.

Don't let your thoughts get away from you. As soon as you have those thoughts that don't line up with God's word, you take them captive. You say to yourself and pray, "It doesn't matter if he is sorry or not. That's the wrong thought to have. God, your Word says we are 'to forgive seventy times seven'. So, I'm choosing to forgive. God, you also say in 1 Corinthians 13:5 NIV that love, '...is not easily angered, it keeps no record of wrongs.' So, I am choosing to replace those thoughts of hopelessness with thoughts of hope. I will not keep a record of wrongs, but I will forgive because Christ has forgiven me, even when I didn't deserve it."

Your enemy is not your husband. While you are devastated by the decision he made, he is not the enemy. We know from Ephesians 6 that we do not wage war in the physical realm against physical things, but in the spiritual. That is why it is important to take your thoughts captive. A popular quote says, "You cannot keep birds from flying over your head, but you can keep them from building a nest in your hair." You can't control whether the thoughts that come into your head are Godly, uplifting thoughts, or if they are negative, damaging thoughts.

But you can control which thoughts stay. You can control if you choose to dwell on the situation, versus battling those thoughts with the Word of God. You can't change the past and you can't control what happens in the future, but you do control your outlook and how you choose to respond.

One helpful way to control your outlook and your response is to have verses to look to so you know exactly how to confront those lies when they enter your head. Let me warn you, our enemy—the devil—is crafty. You are not the first couple that his schemes have threatened to tear apart. I have found so many times that those thoughts that are not God-honoring slip into my mind very subtly. Before I realize it, I'm angry and upset all over again, going down a dangerous path of unforgiveness in my mind. So, stay on guard. 1 Peter 5:8 AMP warns us saying, "Be sober [well balanced and self-disciplined], be alert and cautious at all times. That enemy of yours, the devil, prowls around like a roaring lion [fiercely hungry], seeking someone to devour." While yes, your spouse is under attack, so is your marriage and so are you. Your marriage is important, it is valuable. Stay alert to fight, lest the enemy gets his way, and your marriage is destroyed.

Here are some verses to encourage you and to help you fight the mental battle within when you are ready to give up and sulk. This is what the Bible says about forgiveness:

Matthew 6:12 NIV And forgive us our debts, as we also have forgiven our debtors.

Matthew 6:14 NIV For if you forgive other people when they sin against you, your heavenly Father will also forgive you.

Matthew 6:15 NIV But if you do not forgive others their sins, your Father will not forgive your sins.

Matthew 18:21-22 NIV Then Peter came to Him and asked, "Lord, how many times will my brother sin against me and I forgive him and let it go? Up to seven times?" Jesus answered him, "I say to you, not up to seven times, but seventy times seven.

Matthew 18:35 NIV This is how my heavenly Father will treat each of you unless you forgive your brother or sister from your heart.

Mark 11:25 NIV And when you stand praying, if you hold anything against anyone, forgive them, so that your Father in heaven may forgive you your sins.

Luke 6:37 NIV Do not judge, and you will not be judged. Do not condemn, and you will not be condemned. Forgive, and you will be forgiven.

Luke 17:3-4 NIV So watch yourselves, "If your brother or sister sins against you, rebuke them; and if they repent, forgive them. Even if they sin against you seven times in a day and seven times come back to you say 'I repent,' you must forgive them."

2 Corinthians 2:7 NIV Now instead, you ought to forgive and comfort him, so that he will not be overwhelmed by excessive sorrow.

Ephesians 4:31-32 NIV Get rid of all bitterness, rage and anger, brawling and slander, along with every form of malice. Be kind and compassionate to one another, forgiving each other, just as in Christ God forgave you.

Colossians 3:13 NIV Bear with each other and forgive one another if any of you has a grievance against someone. Forgive as the Lord forgave you.

Having scripture in your mind and heart is always beneficial. In fact, in Psalms 119:11 AMP the Bible says, "Your word I have treasured and stored in my heart, that I may not sin against You." During hardships, these verses take on new life. For instance, what happens if your husband doesn't apologize or he gives you an insincere apology? It can be particularly challenging when you are in a relationship with someone when they are indifferent to your feelings and the apology they offer is nothing but empty words. Even in those times, don't lose sight of what the Bible says about forgiveness. We don't forgive someone based on their behavior. We forgive whether they are really seeking to make things right or not.

I'm not trying to provoke any type of argument between you and your spouse, but when an apology sounds more like lip service, in an appropriate and kind way ask your spouse about it. You could say something like, "Thank you for apologizing, but it sounded very insincere. Was that how you intended it?" Unfortunately, that conversation has happened more than once in our house and it doesn't always revolve around pornography either, as many times it is my husband asking if my apology was sincere. Effective communication, as you'll read more about later, is vital. Since your spouse isn't your enemy, try communicating with that realization in mind. Arguments are going to happen, but when you can stay level-headed in the midst of turmoil, that will do a great deal to disarm the situation.

One last thing I want to add to this section about forgiveness is introspection. This is a concept I want you to keep in mind throughout the entire book. Introspection is the process of looking inside yourself. In this case, we have been talking about forgiving your spouse for some pretty deep wounds they have committed. Unfortunately, we have all sinned at some point in time. Some may make more of a habit than others, but the goal should be holiness. I am still not perfect, and chances are, neither are you. Once again, this is where you may tend to start the comparison game and say, "Well, my failures and struggles aren't as big as his..." Or, my favorite, "This isn't about me—this is about him and his issues." Yes, the porn addiction is a major problem, but let's not lose sight of the shortcomings that might be in your life, too. Chances are, there are things in your life that are not where they are supposed to be.

During the process of healing and working through this issue of pornography, do your best to keep your heart and motives clean. You don't want to enter this process with your actions saying that your spouse needs fixing, but your own issues are no big deal. Introspection is one way to avoid this pitfall. Once again, let me reiterate, porn is a major problem in a relationship, but all sin needs to be dealt with, no matter how big or small. In our relationship with God, all sins have one thing in common, and that is separation from God. Sin may have different physical consequences, but it is all serious. And it isn't fair to expect high standards from your husband while not holding yourself to those same high standards.

God is faithful. He will not leave you or abandon you. Even on the darkest nights when your pain is the greatest, step in faith and forgive your husband. Keep reminding yourself that we are to forgive because we have been forgiven. You are not the Holy Spirit for your spouse. It is not your job to convict or to make him feel guilty for his actions. It is your job to make sure that you are right with God, pray for your spouse, forgive your spouse, and support him on his road to recovery.

I want to close this section with another Pap Elmer story from the war when they were in the Hürtgen Forest in Germany. I'll transcribe the story as he told it, "The 28th got their butts kicked real bad, so we had to go in and relieve them. We took over their foxholes and me and a buddy, Graham, [the subject of our opening story] jumped in and started digging around. They had straw in the fox holes, so we were trying to get settled in and I felt something hard against my back. I reached behind me, and I pulled out a hand grenade, with the pin pulled halfway out. Guess what we did? Put the pin right back in its hole. That hand grenade would have blown us right out of that hole!" He went on to say that the hole was only about 3 feet deep. Just enough to get them below the surface of shots being fired.

So why do I tell that story? Pap was in an extremely dangerous situation. Unbeknownst to him, he landed on a hand grenade that would have killed him unless he acted. Sometimes we can get uncomfortable with a situation and choose to do nothing about it. We keep digging in and squirming around, hoping if we ignore the problem, it will go away. However, if we keep doing that, it can make the situation worse. If Pap kept squirming around and just tried to get comfortable instead of solving the problem, that pin probably would have come out and he would've been killed.

Dealing with forgiveness can be uncomfortable. We don't want confrontation; we just want things to be normal. But they can't be. If we keep ignoring the problem and keep trying to push it away and bury it, it will be fatal. Maybe not physically, but maybe at the expense of your marriage. Instead, do the hard work. Be willing to face the situations and the conversations that make you uncomfortable knowing that facing the problem gives you the power to overcome.

We've discussed forgiveness and I hope that you have seen the importance of forgiving your spouse. Please note though, this isn't a one-time deal. It isn't uncommon for those who are struggling with porn to relapse and view it again and again, and, unfortunately, again. I'm not saying that to discourage you, I'm saying that so you will be prepared. However, no matter how many times it happens, you need to forgive.

I couldn't sleep one night and turned on Christian television. They were playing a clip of Joyce Meyer discussing forgiveness between herself and her husband. She mentioned that they work from the mentality that they had already decided they were going to forgive the other, so they didn't spend time staying mad because they already knew they were going to be forgiving the other person in the relationship.

Sadly, I see a lot of relationships that are not like that. They decide after the fact as to whether they are going to forgive. I can see how always forgiving may scare some people. Some may be concerned that if you are that forgiving that maybe your husband will take advantage of that fact and keep on doing what he's doing. Well, he might. But no matter his actions, it doesn't change our Biblical mandate to forgive. Remember forgiveness doesn't mean there are not consequences and it doesn't mean you are ignoring the issue at hand. You can forgive, but still proceed cautiously. You can forgive, but still look for ways to help your husband. I admonish you to leave the mentality of selective forgiveness, instead adopt one that is to always forgive, no matter the offense.

4.

The Truth About Emotions

So, let's talk emotions. Every woman and situation is different, but one thing is certain: the emotional side of this addiction is not full of joyous emotions. Personally, I experienced sadness, disappointment, frustration, and hopelessness the most. Disappointment happens when expectations aren't met. And in the case of a porn addiction, marital expectations are definitely not met. When it comes to handling negative emotions, how should those be handled from a Christian perspective? Does the Bible have any guidance on the matter?

Addiction aside, how many people do you know who are overflowing with joy? How many Christians do you know that are radiating joy and peace from God? Do you see that? Or do you see more of people…struggling. It's like there's a cloud over them in which they can't get out of its shadow. Like most people, I have social media accounts and I'm sure much like you, I see different posts from different people in my list of friends handling situations in a variety of ways. One common way I see people "handle" things is by having almost a passive-aggressive post about how they have to smile when they are hurting on the inside, and how they never wear their feelings on their sleeves. Here's the thing: we've all had those situations. We've all had to go through negative experiences or negative emotions without many people around us knowing how we are feeling. It makes me sad to think that many people's true mood would be despair if they didn't have to be "so strong" for those around them. Is that how we are supposed to live? Of course not! It doesn't mean that we do not have temporary seasons of sadness, but our overall emotional center should be peace and joy.

I don't mean this as a criticism in any way, but rather as a hand out to show how you can rise above the despair, rise above the emotions, to rise above all of those things, and walk as your nature as a true child of God. As a believer, you are not meant to walk in defeat. Think about it, who is happier, the people who won or the people who lost? That's right, the people who won! The losing side walks around sulking, not the victorious ones. You, as a Christian, are to walk in victory, and the victorious are joyous. I know that may be a tough perspective to have when you're dealing with the emotions involved with your spouse's porn addiction, but you can get to that point where you walk in victory and joy no matter what is going on around you. Let's get started!

First, I want to talk about the disappointment and sadness that commonly accompanies a spousal porn addiction. I've had plenty of chances to let things get me down, aside from Johnnie's struggles. During the process of writing this book, we experienced the miscarriage of our 4th child, we've lost four grandparents, had extended family issues to work through, and had the sudden loss of all income. I'm not trying to play a comparison game so you can figure out how hurt you are compared to me, but rather offering those examples so you know that we have had things in our life that have been almost devastating. Especially going through the miscarriage, and even though we were mourning, we didn't let our loss dominate everything. With the addiction you are dealing with in your family, I urge to you the same thing, don't let it dominate everything. It's okay to be sad and disappointed, but you also can't let that be where you set up your tent and stay.

How do you have joy amid all the sorrow? How do you have peace during chaos and uncertainty? How do you deal with all the frustration? Medication isn't the answer, a passive-aggressive social media post is not the answer, and binge watching your favorite show is not the answer, either. Only one thing can bring change, and that is your relationship with the Lord. It's sad to think that many Christians don't believe what the Bible says. They are quick to talk to their friends, but they don't apply that same zeal in taking their supplications to the feet of the one who can change their life.

In times of hardship, you must go back to what the Bible says. What does the Bible say about joy? We're going to start in the Old Testament, those were the years before Christ was born. Things were rough back then. There was no running water, no bathrooms, no aluminum foil, and no hot water heaters. More importantly, they didn't have the Holy Spirit in the way we are able to receive today because there was not a redemptive covenant yet. The Holy Spirit would come on people at different times, but He didn't fill people like He does today.

Their only hope was living by faith and obeying the law.

Yep. The Old Testament law, a long list of dos and don'ts. The list was pretty much impossible except for one man, Jesus. But, at this time in history, Jesus had not come.

In Nehemiah 8:10 NLT the Bible says, "The joy of the Lord is your strength." That verse flows easily off the tongue, and I know it's the perfect verse you find on mugs and t-shirts, but what does it really mean? We've already talked about some of those passive-aggressive social media posts, so I'm not necessarily convinced by your mug, so let's keep going and figure out what joy is all about. If you break it down, it's saying that there is something so unique about the joy the Lord offers, that it can be your strength.

To offer a little more context to this verse, I'm going to tell you more about the book of Nehemiah. At this point in the history of Israel, some of the Israelites had returned from captivity and they were starting the process of rebuilding the walls of Jerusalem, roughly 445 BC. Nehemiah, Ezra, and the priests began to read the law (Genesis-Deuteronomy) to the people. This was the first time the Israelites had heard the law in a long time, and they realized how far they were from the standards that were set by God, and they began to cry. The whole reason they were in captivity in the first place was because they hadn't obeyed God. The priests and Nehemiah stopped reading and told the people to stop crying! And this is where the famous verse makes its debut. "For the joy of the Lord is your strength!" As the priests were trying to calm the people down and explain the law to them, eventually the people went their way full of joy because they understood what had been made known to them in the law. They heard, they understood, then they wanted change.

This passage in Nehemiah is important for everyone

today. You have a group of people who are sad because they haven't been doing what they should have been doing. Now, this probably isn't just personal remorse, because if you have read some of the earlier books in the Bible you would also understand that the obedience of the Israelites to the law has its effects in how families are blessed and prospered. Because of their disobedience, they have a lot to be sad about. However, as they gained understanding from the Word of God, their disposition changed. No longer were they grieved, but they were joyous. I think one reason for their joy is because they had hope.

The verses following describe how the men of the households came back the following day to hear more of the law and to gain more understanding. When we have an understanding of what the Bible says and how to apply it, it can change our lives, no matter the situation. As it specifically relates to this matter, we know we can have joy in the middle of perilous times because we know there is something unique about our relationship with God through which He provides joy for us.

1 Chronicles 16:27 AMP also has an interesting verse about joy. It says, "Splendor and majesty are [found] in His presence; strength and joy are [found] in His place (sanctuary)." The Hebrew word for joy used in this verse is the only other time this specific word for joy is used besides the passage in Nehemiah 8 mentioned above. This tells me there is something different about this word since there are numerous other passages that mention joy. The Hebrew word is *chedva*. This particular type of joy means "pure and unfiltered, expressing the happiness of being with others."[1]

Another commentator broke down the Hebrew word by picture. This may sound odd if you aren't familiar with the

Hebrew language, but the characters in their alphabet have associations with different pictures by which you can derive a meaning. This commentator noted how *chedva* is related to the word for a door in a wall or fence. And when taken into consideration with the verse it can be taken to mean the joy that comes with entering "through the door" to be in covenant with the Lord.[2] It goes right back to the original definition—the joy of being together. As Christians, we are so fortunate that part of our relationship with Christ comes a joy that can give us strength because we are in a relationship with Him.

As we continue through the Old Testament, let's look at Psalm 16:11 AMP . The Bible says, "You will show me the path of life; In Your presence is fullness of joy; In Your right hand there are pleasures forevermore." We have heard the verse, and now we need to understand this verse. What's the verse saying? The verse is saying that there is fullness of joy in God's presence, which goes back to the verse we just read in 1 Chronicles. There is something about being in the presence of God that changes things. We may know that from our experiences in the presence of God, but bigger than our experiences is that we have the Word of God telling us that in God's presence, there is fullness of joy.

With the onslaught of negative emotions you may be experiencing regarding your spouse, spending time in God's presence is imperative. How do you get into God's presence here on Earth? Well, the Bible makes that process pretty simple, too. In Psalms 100 we are to enter into His gates with thanksgiving and into His courts with praise. You can do this in prayer. It's simply telling God how great He is and how thankful you are for the things He has done for you. Yes, you might be more focused on the sadness and desperation you are experiencing, but take a moment in prayer and tell God things you are thankful for.

One easy way for me is to turn on some praise and worship music. I know it can be hard trying to figure out what song to listen to, but listen to something that glorifies God, not your problems. It can be in your room, in your living room, in your car, or outside. It isn't limited to the four walls of the church. I can't emphasize this enough because I know it works from my own experiences, but the Bible also says it and it's the absolute authority. To get in the presence of the Lord you enter by praise and worship. When you are singing, don't just sing slow songs about how hard life is, or lyrics that state maybe God will help one day. No, instead sing songs full of faith and victory, grounded in the Word of God. It will encourage you and you will find joy and hope coming to you.

The next verse is Isaiah 61:3 AMP which says, " To grant to those who mourn in Zion the following: To give them a turban instead of dust [on their heads, a sign of mourning], The oil of joy instead of mourning, The garment [expressive] of praise instead of a disheartened spirit. So they will be called the trees of righteousness [strong and magnificent, distinguished for integrity, justice, and right standing with God], The planting of the Lord, that He may be glorified." This is a part of a great passage of scripture at the beginning of chapter 61:1-3. In verse three above it mentions the oil of joy and the garment of praise. Here we have it again—praise and joy are together. Are you beginning to notice a trend? The first two verses from this passage are quoted by Jesus in Luke 4 who says that these words from Isaiah are fulfilled in Him. These verses are saying, once again, that the Lord is our source of joy. He doesn't want us to be in despair or faint in heart. Not only does He not want us that way, but we don't EVER have to stay that way!

So why oil? Oil was commonly used for festive things like celebrations. The lack of use of oil was indicative of being in mourning. This adds another layer of meaning to this verse. The time of mourning is over! You have something to rejoice about. No, life may not be perfect. You may be feeling like there is no end in sight to what your husband is dealing with. But just because the circumstances around you aren't ideal, it doesn't mean you have to walk in sadness.

When we had the miscarriage in 2019, I wasn't expecting it at all. We had 3 other pregnancies with no problems. The day the bleeding started it really caught me off guard. By the end of the day, we had lost our baby. It was early in the pregnancy, so we don't really know how long he survived in my womb, but by that night, he was gone. My body delivered him. I was so upset. Johnnie and I both were. We handled it in different ways, but we were both upset. We both shed tears. It was very hard on me, but then one day, I believe it was the very next day, something remarkable happened.

I was eating breakfast and our youngest, who was around 18 months, pitched a fit about something and it made me realize I would never get to have that experience with the baby I lost. With that realization, I began to cry. I excused myself to the bedroom to turn on some music and pray. I knew the exact song I wanted to listen to. So, I clicked on the album and the specific song I wanted to hear, but rather than the song I selected, a different song began to play from the album. The words that rang out in one of my most difficult seasons was a song by Eddie James that says, " I just declare that what you've sown in tears you will reap in joy; He's turning your mourning into dancing; He's turning your sorrow into joy..."[3]

It was only the Lord. In that moment of grief, it was

a reminder that the Lord's joy was still there. He was still turning mourning into dancing. What I was sowing in tears, I would reap in joy. Which is Psalm 126:5-6. You can have the same thing. I know you have sown some tears regarding your husband and the future of your marriage. It hurts, I know it does! But, even in the tough times when you have more questions than answers, you can be filled with the joy, peace, and hope that comes from the Lord.

Let's look at Romans 15:13. The Old Testament pairs joy and peace together a lot. In the New Testament, you hear a lot about joy and the Holy Spirit. The Holy Spirit is God. Just as God filled people with joy in the Old Testament, so it is in the New Testament. We have joy as a result of the Holy Spirit living inside of us. Romans 15:13 NLT says, "I pray that God, the source of hope, will fill you completely with joy and peace because you trust in him. Then you will overflow with confident hope through the power of the Holy Spirit." So in this passage, we read that God will fill us with all joy as we trust Him. And through the power of the Holy Spirit we will abound with hope and confidence in His promises. Some of those promises involve joy. We will have joy in His presence, we will be strong because of His joy, and we will be expressive with our joy if we are living by the Spirit.

So, what's the problem with joy? There is no problem. The problem is that many people don't have continual joy in their lives. But, it doesn't have to be that way. Your emotions don't have to dominate you, you can continually experience the joy of the Lord no matter what life brings. It is a gift from the Lord, part of our nature in Christ.

In the New Testament, we read about the fruit of the Spirit in Galatians 5. Paul gives a long list of the result of living by the flesh, then he gives a list of attributes that are the result of living by the Spirit. In that list, we find many qualities that can help during disappointment. Love, joy, peace, patience, kindness, goodness, gentleness, faithfulness, and self-control. Look at that list, we need ALL of those while dealing with the addiction, don't we? Not just that, we need those attributes just to go to the store! And how do you get them? By living by the Spirit. Which then begs the question, how do you live by the Spirit?

Reading through Galatians 5 you will read many verses about what walking by the Spirit looks like, as opposed to walking in the flesh. As Galatians explains it, you know you are walking by the Spirit when you aren't doing the actions of the flesh. Meaning, you aren't acting in sinful ways that are not God-like. Verse 16 AMP says, "But I say, walk habitually in the [Holy] Spirit [seek Him and be responsive to His guidance], and then you will certainly not carry out the desire of the sinful nature [which responds impulsively without regard for God and His precepts]." Then in verse 25 it says, "If we [claim to] live by the [Holy] Spirit, we must also walk by the Spirit [with personal integrity, godly character, and moral courage—our conduct empowered by the Holy Spirit].

Do you need more joy in your life? Search the Bible and then live by the Spirit. Do you need more gentleness? Search the Word of God for understanding, then seek to live by the Spirit. Just as it was in the book of Nehemiah, once the people understood the Law they could begin to do the things it said. When you understand what the Bible says about joy or peace—whatever fruit you are thinking of—you then have the ability to start walking it out.

The key to all of this is the Word of God, the Bible. Read it and then do it. You cannot medicate yourself enough, you cannot go on enough vacations, you cannot watch enough episodes of your favorite show—nothing will help your emotions long term except the Lord. Which finally brings me to the book of John.

John 14 AMP has a famous passage in verse one, "Do not let your heart be troubled (afraid, cowardly). Believe [confidently] in God and trust in Him, [have faith, hold on to it, rely on it, keep going and] believe also in Me." I want to zero in on that first statement: "Do not let your heart be troubled." Yes, Jesus was referencing the feelings his disciples were experiencing in relation to his crucifixion and the aftermath, but he said something crucial, do not LET your heart be troubled. Meaning, you can control when your heart is troubled. You may not be able to control what circumstances may come—for instance, if your friend and leader is about to be crucified—but you can control if your heart is troubled. Or, as the Amplified Version words it, "afraid, cowardly".

How many times have you heard that in your life? Probably not many. Especially now in this era, it is all about exploring your feelings and not being afraid to feel your feelings and following the path they are leading you, claiming them as your identity, no matter its ethical or spiritual conclusion. But here we have it, straight from Jesus that we can let our hearts not be troubled.

The usage of the word "troubled" is just as you think it would mean. It can mean troubled, to agitate, to trouble (a thing, by the movement of its parts to and fro), to cause one inward commotion, take away his calmness of mind, make restless, to stir up, to strike one's spirit with fear and dread, to render anxious or distressed, to perplex the mind of one by suggesting scruples or doubts. Strong's Concordance definition

49

says to stir or agitate (roil water). In all honesty, I had no idea what "roil" meant. I wasn't sure if it was a typo or not, and it turns out it isn't. The word roil means to muddy the water by agitating the sediment.

Now that you know what the word roil means, it provides such a clear picture of that verse. Most of us have been walking through a creek, lake, or some other body of water and witnessed what happens when the sediment gets stirred up. The once clear water becomes muddy. This muddiness is what can happen within our hearts. Strong's explains that our hearts can figuratively mean our thoughts, feelings, and mind. Our hearts, just like the water in a stream, can be serene and clear. Then something is said or thought that begins to stir up the sediment and muddy the waters.

For instance, your husband could tell you that he has slipped up again. Or perhaps, you find a porn stash you didn't know about. Or maybe you can just tell that things aren't right between the two of you. Honestly, it doesn't even have to be porn related. You could be afraid. You could be angry; you could be upset or worried. You could be sad and stressed. Those types of emotions and feelings are common among all of us. On any given day we can experience all of those.

A survey that was reported in 2017 showed that there was a 65% increase in antidepressant usage between 1999-2014.[4] I'm not trying to pick on people who take antidepressants, but I'm just trying to show proof that there are troubled hearts. And while I'm thankful that we have had so many medicinal advances, it does show what is going on. Now, I can already hear the nay-sayers. "Depression is a sickness; it can be a chemical imbalance. It has nothing to do with spirituality!" Hear me now, I'm not saying it isn't a sickness. But what I AM saying is don't jump to the medicine cabinet—or the TV cabinet—and attempt to self-medicate and escape before you take your troubled, muddled thoughts and hearts to the One who created you. There is no better way to clear the muddy heart than to introduce truth.

So, what do you do when all these negative emotions are flooding your mind? You feel hopeless, sad, depressed, and unsure of the future. You introduce the truth of the Bible. As you read this book, you will be reading a lot of the Bible. We have been through some very tumultuous times, and every time it has been our reliance on the Bible that has made the difference. Even when your marriage isn't going the way you expected and you don't know what is going to happen next, know that you can face any situation successfully as long as you are standing on what the Bible says.

None of us are immune to hurt and pain. It doesn't matter how tough an exterior you try to display, hurt will happen and it's okay. It's okay to love your husband and it's okay to show that you are upset by the wrong that has been done. There comes a time when you need to move from hurt to forgiveness and then from forgiveness to start the process of healing. I've seen it far too often when people get so caught up in their pain or emotional state that it becomes a part of their perceived identity.

No longer are they the victorious one, but the one who has labeled themselves as not loved, not wanted, or the worrier. Typical for our enemy, the devil, it is very subtle. I notice it because I too did the same thing. For much of my teenage life, I felt I wasn't pretty. I had mentally labeled myself as such and my mindset began to control my actions. Even as Johnnie has struggled with porn, my first thought was: I must not be pretty enough. And just like that, the mental myths began to take root in my mind.

When your spouse struggles, you will likely take a self-esteem hit, I know I did. You can forgive your spouse, but then immediately start self-labeling in an attempt to cover your hurt. Let me remind you, as I needed to remind myself, that we are not to put any label on ourselves that does not come from God Almighty. You may be tempted to say negative things about your looks, your emotional state, your size—the list goes on and on. But the Word of God has powerful things to say about you too, and it has nothing to do with whether your emotions are in a tailspin or if you are tipping the scale more than you would like to. It is solely based on your position in Christ as a Christian, and this knowledge is crucial in this fight. Knowing who you are in Christ and what the Bible says about you is the best place to start when you are beginning to process your emotions and feelings about what is going on in your marriage.

I was given a paper that listed all the verses of who I am in Christ and I was told that I needed to say those things out loud at least once a day until I knew them. I am not going to provide an exhaustive list, but I encourage you to look one up. You can easily find them online. But I do want to highlight a few.

1. You are more than a conqueror. "Who shall ever separate us from the love of Christ? Will tribulation, or distress, or persecution, or famine, or nakedness, or danger, or sword? Yet in all these things we are more than conquerors and gain an overwhelming victory through Him who loved us so much that He died for us." Romans 8:35, 37 AMP.

First of all, these verses are not talking about conquering your husband. These verses in Romans give a long list of things that some might think would separate us from the love of God (distress, tribulation, famine, persecution, etc.), then in verse 37 it says we are more than conquerors and we have the overwhelming victory! So, it doesn't matter the situation with your husband. Whether he's looking at porn once a day, once a week, or once a month, you do not have to be conquered by your feelings and emotions or defeat or low self-worth. You will not be hopeless in this struggle, but hopeful because God is on your side and we are more than conquerors. When you feel defeated in your fight for your husband, your prayers change and you start feeling hopeless, but my friend remember, we serve the God of hope (Romans 15:13). There is NOTHING He cannot do.

2. You have the mind of Christ. "For who has known the mind and purposes of the Lord, so as to instruct Him? But we have the mind of Christ [to be guided by His thoughts and purposes]." 1 Corinthians 2:16 AMP

As with all things in the Christian life, having the mind of Christ doesn't happen automatically. We have it available to us, but until we put that knowledge into action, it can lay dormant. In our position in Christ, we have the mind of Christ, as in we don't have to be led by our sinful nature or by others, but we also have the mind of Christ "to be guided by His thoughts and purposes", as the Amplified version explains. Meaning, when those hurtful, doubtful, unforgiving, frustrated, etc., thoughts come into our mind, we are not held captive by them. Instead, we can say, "I have the mind of Christ. Christ is not hurtful, doubtful, or unforgiving and neither am I." We can renew our determination to fight the mental battle and to take thoughts captive, as we have already discussed, because we have the mind of Christ. We are guided by His thoughts and purposes.

3. You have the peace of God. "Do not be anxious or worried about anything, but in everything [every circumstance and situation] by prayer and petition with thanksgiving, continue to make your [specific] requests known to God. And the peace of God [that peace which reassures the heart, that peace] which transcends all understanding, [that peace which] stands guard over your hearts and your minds in Christ Jesus [is yours]." Philippians 4:7-8 AMP

You may not feel peaceful when your emotions are in turmoil. Or when you are mulling over what your husband might be doing while you are out of the house. But luckily, you can depend on the peace of God that is yours. This peace, however, comes at a time when you have prayed over the situation and let go of the anxious and worrisome thoughts (verse 6). A quick note about the "with thanksgiving" clause it mentions. I don't think it is implying that you should be thankful that your husband is looking at pornography. But rather thankful that God is in the midst of the situation with you. And thankful that by the grace of God, you will see a change come to your family. That portion aside, it's important as you are praying and ridding yourself of these anxious thoughts, you realize you can stand firm knowing the peace of God is yours.

4. You are His workmanship. "For we are His workmanship [His own master work, a work of art], created in Christ Jesus [reborn from above—spiritually transformed, renewed, ready to be used] for good works, which God prepared [for us] beforehand [taking paths which He set], so that we would walk in them [living the good life which He prearranged and made ready for us]." Ephesians 2:10 AMP

It can be very tempting to look down on yourself during this time. Whether it has something you have done, how you look, etc. It is easy to lose sight of the fact that you are the workmanship of God. He made you, He fabricated you. You are not a mistake. When the thoughts enter your head promoting the opposite, just remember that you are the workmanship of God. Not only does this verse call you a work of art, but God has created you for good works prepared before the foundations of the world. You are not here by accident. While your circumstances are frustrating and I wish you didn't have to go through it, it doesn't change how God looks at you.

Those are only a few verses from a long list of your identity in Christ. But let's not lose the fact that the same identity you have in Christ, is the same identity your husband has as well. This is a tough time for you, but this is tough for him, too. Your husband is not your enemy. As much as you have to battle thoughts in your mind, remember he is not the enemy.

Your recovery and healing from this wound doesn't happen overnight, but it can happen over time. You don't have to live with this pain for the rest of your life. But it starts with processing the situation. Meaning, you need to know the facts and understand your husband's side of the story. No doubt, you are experiencing a wide variety of emotions and asking yourself a lot of questions. How long has this been going on? Is he going to change? Does he want to change? There were thoughts I had that I wasn't sure how to think through them, and I had questions that I wasn't sure how to answer. Truth be told, some I didn't want to know the answer. Eventually, I got the nerve to talk to my husband about some of these questions and I realized the answers weren't nearly as scary as I thought they might be.

Knowing the truth helped me begin to heal because I had some misconceptions that were attributing to my pain. In the next chapters, we are going to talk about some of those questions I had and some that maybe you have had. Hopefully, you will have a different understanding of the struggle your husband is up against. It's always helpful to know that we are not alone in this struggle and that some of the same thoughts you have had are being had by other women.

Truth is a powerful thing. In John 8:32 NLT, it says, "And you will know the truth and the truth will set you free." As Christians, when we know the Truth, which is Jesus, we can dispel the lies and the strongholds of the enemy. We can be totally free. This principle relates not only to spiritual matters but also to our personal lives. When we are armed with truth, we can dismantle the lies that entangle us. I was believing some lies. I thought that Johnnie's porn addiction had more to do with me, that maybe he didn't really love me, and that he hadn't changed like I thought he had. What questions are you having in your mind? Are they truths or lies? We are going to explore some of the most common mindsets when dealing with a spouse who has a porn addiction. You will be able to see whether they are truths, lies, or if they fall somewhere in between.

Notes:

1.https://www.tbs-online.org/rabbi-perlins-study/simcha
joy-one-favorite-jewish-values-october-2015-kol/
2. http://hethathasanear.com/Joy.html
3. https://genius.com/Eddie-james-joy-lyrics
4. https://consumer.healthday.com/mental-health-infor-
mation-25/antidepressants-news-723/u-s-antidepres-
sant-use-jumps-65-percent-in-15-years-725586.html

5.

It's Me...Isn't It?

I t's time to explore some different mindsets that you may be having. Knowing the truth is vital, and recognizing and expelling lies is a crucial step in that direction. So, let's start with the first, arguably most prominent thought that many women may ask themselves.

1. I'm not pretty enough and my body isn't the right proportions.

In struggling with self-esteem issues for so long, when Johnnie told me he was looking at porn again, I reverted instantly to thinking it was my fault because I wasn't...enough. I wasn't pretty enough, I wasn't skinny enough, I wasn't tan enough. You've been there, right? The questions never stop coming. When he first told me, we hadn't been married long and I was in decent shape, physically. My love handles had a little more "love" than I wanted them to, but overall, I was thin. I have always been pale-skinned, and in my mind, pale wasn't as complimentary as someone who has a nice tan. I fell into the trap of scrutinizing every part of me. And it can be hard not to. Hearing all my life that men are visual, it was extremely easy to deduce that if men are visual and if they don't like what they see, then they will look elsewhere.

Now, my new husband was looking elsewhere. Seems logical, right? Well, it may be logical, but that doesn't mean it is correct. However, Johnnie has assured me time after time that it has nothing to do with my looks. Maybe your husband has told you the same thing. I had trouble believing and understanding that concept, but the more I thought about it, and the more I learned about it, the more I could see his perspective. I began to understand that I didn't drive him to pornography and there were times it was used more as a coping mechanism, so, his reasoning was making some sense.

Your husband married you for a reason, and one of those reasons is that he loves you. If he was never attracted to you, then you probably wouldn't have been married. I understand bodies change over the years. You may be carrying around more weight than you would like, or you may have started to wrinkle, but that doesn't mean that your husband isn't committed to you. And you can't base whether he is attracted to you based on his behaviors as it is related to porn. It is extremely dangerous to assume something when the whole picture isn't seen.

The women my husband looked at are probably prettier than I am. When we got married, our ability to discern whether we are physically attracted to someone did not get turned off. Johnnie and I have both said that when we got married, on some level we thought that we would never notice the attractiveness of the opposite sex. That is not true. You still encounter other people. Noticing someone is attractive doesn't mean you don't love your spouse. But you do need to know to bounce your eyes away when you know you may be tempted to look and linger.

With Johnnie, pornography started off as a fantasy. He saw all these other women before he saw me. While I was thinking that my features drove him to porn, that wasn't the case. His fantasies existed before me. Even though he had those images in his head, it didn't make him any more or less attracted to me. We know from watching the rich and famous that being married to a supermodel doesn't make men immune to seeing other attractive women. So, it's not your fault. You are not responsible for his decisions. As you will see when we explore some of the statistics of pornography, you will find that chances are, your husband's fantasies probably existed before the two of you were married, too.

Johnnie is incredibly open and forthcoming with information about the guy's side of the struggle. One thing I have learned is that as hard as it is for me to understand the role of attraction your spouse plays; it is equally hard for him to explain it. In attempting to explain it, he compared it to cars. Now, part of this analogy sounds awful, but bear with me until the end and it will make sense. Yes, we are comparing relationships to cars, but, no, we are not saying that some women are Ferraris and others are minivans. Supercars are exotic and incredibly attractive. But those who own supercars have said, you don't want one for your everyday driver. They are fast, and they look good, but you don't want to live with them. They overheat in traffic, can't go over speed bumps, they are hard to get in and out of, and they're expensive. Some of their tires cost thousands of dollars per tire, and don't think about leaving the car out in public, or someone may try to take it or damage it. (See, it sounds awful at this point, doesn't it?)

When it comes to porn, men don't actually want to be with that person in the picture or movie. It's only for looks and momentary pleasure. She isn't the person he wants to live life with. Some men have tried. They have an affair, get a divorce, and marry their mistress, only to be looking for someone else shortly thereafter because they realize that looks are not what completes the relationship. This echoes what Proverbs 31:30 NLT says, "Charm is deceptive, and beauty does not last; but a woman who fears the Lord will be greatly praised." Just as consumers can be deceived into thinking that owning a supercar can fulfill their desires, so men can be deceived into thinking that pornography can fulfill their desires.

We may never fully understand a man's addiction to porn, but chances are, your looks and proportions are not the things that are driving your husband to porn. Are porn stars pretty? Eh, some are, some aren't (so I'm told). But your husband could say the same about you. This pornography addiction is not about you. Sometimes it is nothing more than a fantasy. A porn addiction can also stem from pride in your husband's life, his desire for control, or wanting to self-medicate. Yes, it is always wrong, but don't blame your looks or proportions.

I realize this doesn't apply to everyone, but sometimes it is easy to relax into the mindset of: "We're married, so I get to stop trying!" Ladies don't stop trying to attract your husband. When you and your husband were dating or maybe you had just met and were starting your relationship, you both probably did things to make the other person more attracted to you. For instance, you didn't go everywhere in your baggiest pair of sweatpants, but maybe a nice pair of jeans or shorts. Your husband probably showered before you guys went on a date and didn't show up sweaty and gross. You did those things to put your best foot forward.

Now that you are married, don't lose sight of those standards. Not the standards in and of themselves, but the excitement that led you to want to put on some make-up or dress up a little more. You did it because you were excited about your significant other and you wanted them to be attracted to you. If you have lost some of that excitement, think back to when you were dating and how excited you were to be together. Take some time to remember that God created the two of you to be together. Take some time to remember the good things about your marriage. And, if the situation warrants it, take some extra time to dress up a little. Or trade in your baggy sweatpants for a pair of jeans. Just because you are married doesn't mean you quit trying to attract your spouse. Put some effort into putting your best foot forward.

Please understand what I am saying and don't go to the extreme. For instance, we have 4 kids and there are days when make-up doesn't get applied, where I'm in my sweatpants and T-shirt all day, and looking pretty frumpy. Johnnie understands that. But I don't make a habit of it. Your marriage relationship is important, act like it!

Trying to communicate this concept can be complicated. I never want a woman to feel like if her husband ever sees her frumpy, then he may go look at porn—I'm not implying that at all. Nor am I saying that if you are always looking your best, your husband will never look at porn again. Saying either statement would mean that you, the woman, are to blame for your husband's actions and that is simply not the case. I'll say it again—your looks are not to blame. What I do want to ensure that you know from this section is that it is important for both you and your husband to keep trying to attract each other. Why? One reason is that it demonstrates to you both that the relationship is important, you are important, and your marriage has value.

With that being said, there are instances where men are so deeply addicted to pornography and masturbation that they don't want to change and would rather leave the relationship. Some have said they aren't attracted to their spouse anymore and want to make their fantasies a reality. While this isn't common, it does happen. How to cope with your husband when he doesn't want to change is something we will be discussing further in a later chapter.

I'm not pretty enough: FALSE

#2 Marriage isn't worth the fight. Isn't he basically committing adultery, anyway?

At what point do you give up? At what point do you say, enough is enough, I'm done. My answer: never. I asked Johnnie at what point in our marriage would he divorce me, he looked at me and said, "I said until death." (Speaking of our wedding vows).

The subject of this book is sexual failure. I don't want to get into an ethical or biblical debate as to when to flee a dangerous situation or anything of that nature. But we do need to discuss your end game. What is your purpose? Are you committed to seeing your marriage through until death do you part? Or does the commitment end sometime before that?

I realize that some of you may have already been through a divorce, so your history may make you view this a little differently. Whether it is yourself or you are looking to your friends and family, it doesn't take long to find someone who has had a divorce. They may be remarried now, but looking through my list of friends and family, it seems common to hear. Trying to understand updated statistics of divorce can be complicated since those figures are measured in about four different ways. One thing we can surmise from those statistics is that divorce is a big problem.

Seeing so many people who have come before us ending their marriage, it is easy to think of that as an option. But just because a large swath of the population has done that, it doesn't make it right. One article I read stated that, "62 percent of exes said they wished their spouses had worked harder to stay married. Thirty-five percent of men and 21 percent of women said they wished they, themselves, had worked harder in their marriage." [1] So don't give up! Don't be one of those statistics that looks back thinking that you wish you would have worked harder to save your marriage.

One evening I was driving home and painted on the rear window of the car in front of me said:

"Finally divorced! Honk if ya feel me!"

We were stopped at a red light, so I took a picture of it because I didn't think anyone would believe me otherwise. Now, I don't know the circumstances of that marriage. It could've been an adulterous or abusive situation. But the message was still sobering. Marriage isn't a commitment that is respected like it used to be.

Despite the messages sent by culture, remember that marriage is important! Fighting for your marriage is important! God cares so much about marriage faithfulness because it is a picture of His love for us. He sealed His love with a promise, and that was the blood of Jesus. We are in a covenant relationship with Him because of the blood of Jesus. Our earthly marriages mirror that covenant. If we aren't faithful in our relationship or sex lives, it is easy to fall into the trap that God won't be faithful either, even thinking that God would go back on his promise, which isn't true. God will never do that. Our marriages are a picture of that. I think that is one reason Satan is attacking sexuality, purity, and marriage so much. It's because it is a picture of God's relationship with us.

Marriage is a God-ordained relationship and a picture of our relationship with God. The book of Genesis speaks of marriage joining the husband and wife together and becoming one. In Jesus' teaching on marriage and divorce in Matthew and in Mark we read, "Therefore, what God has joined together, let no one separate." By far, one of my favorite lines in a wedding ceremony. We know from that verse that God has joined man and wife together—God, not ourselves. And marriages are not to separate.

If you know your Bible you may think about how Moses allowed for divorces, but if you read the context, it was because the Israelites had hard hearts. It wasn't God's original plan. (Matthew 19:8) He didn't design marriage to be something that comes and goes like a passing fad. He made it to last. Even when we are frustrated and mad, it is to last. You are one with your husband. You can't spiritually or physically undo your commitment. Don't give up. Even on the tough days, trust that God can get you through this time.

Jesus says in Matthew 5:27 & 28 that if a man looks lustfully at a woman, he has already committed adultery in his heart. But, read carefully, the passage say "in his heart". This does not mean that your husband has physically violated your marriage covenant, but that he has a heart problem. He has sin in his heart, and there is a chance that you do, too. This verse has shock value, but it would also mean that any time either of you had a lustful thought, it was grounds for divorce, and I don't think that is what Jesus is advocating. In fact, 4 verses later is when Jesus says the only reason for divorce is sexual immorality.

It is an interesting progression reading verses 27-32 of Matthew chapter 5. It begins discussing lustful thoughts, then it moves on to say that if your hands or eyes cause you to sin, get rid of them! After that, it progresses to divorcing for sexual immorality reasons only. As if to say, lustful looking is wrong, and it is sin. You need to stop sinning, or it will escalate from something that is in your heart to something committed by your body which can have permanent effects. So yes, it is serious, but this verse is not advocating that you throw in the towel on your marriage.

Hosea, the Biblical prophet who was married to a prostitute, had some dark days in his marriage too. If there is any Biblical character that can relate to having an unfaithful spouse, Hosea is our guy! We are going to delve into his story later, because no matter where you are in your marriage, there is something to learn from his story of faithfulness.

Marriage is not worth the fight: FALSE

#3 We don't have enough sex—that's why he looks at pornography.

Sex is important in a marriage relationship. You may hear couples say they don't have sex as much the longer they are married. While that may be common to hear, it doesn't mean that is the way it has to be or the way it is supposed to be. One thing that does affect your sex life is your relationship with your spouse. Let's look at a scenario: For one reason or another a woman doesn't have sex with her husband, and this becomes a fairly standard thing. Eventually, the husband gets frustrated, and his outlet is porn. Thus, the woman then thinks that her husband's porn obsession is her fault. Let's break this down.

First, as we mentioned earlier, you are not responsible for your husband's actions. He is responsible for what he does. If you are not having sex often, he should have the self-discipline to be able to control himself.

However, if you find that you are habitually not having sex, you need to look at the root of those feelings. What is leading to these feelings in the first place? Are you too tired? Is he being inconsiderate in other areas of your relationship? Are you self-conscious? Are you unhappy?

While your husband should have self-control, it is unfair for you to withhold sex from him. I am NOT saying that you have to agree to it every time no matter how you feel. Rather I am saying that if you know there is a pattern as to why you never feel like having sex, you need to talk about it and start doing what you can to rectify what is separating you.

For instance, if you find that you are too tired, try having a cup of coffee or getting some rest earlier in the day. However, if you find that your husband is being inconsiderate in other areas of your relationship and that is leading to a lack of intimacy, you must communicate about that. In the next section we are going to talk about communication and some of those same principles will apply. Either way, if there is something keeping you from being intimate with your spouse, it needs to be exposed. I can't promise how things will turn out, but if you don't make an effort to see things change, then they won't change. If a lack of intimacy is present in your marriage, I'm sure your spouse is concerned about it and would like to see a change.

When you know that your husband is struggling with porn, it is hard not to be self-conscious. And it's hard not to let that self-consciousness lead to a lack of intimacy. I know I was comparing myself to an internet-ideal woman. I don't know what exactly Johnnie was looking at, but I was fairly sure my looks were different. It was hard to overcome, but that's when I had to realize that while I was self-conscious, I didn't have to stay that way. It was at that time I had to realize, once again, that it wasn't my looks that drove him to pornography.

I think back to the book of Genesis in the Bible where Adam and Eve were naked and unashamed. (Genesis 2:25) While that instance was before the fall into sin, I still think that is a level of intimacy you can and should experience with your spouse. Two things that have helped me combat those insecure feelings are (1) Johnnie and I communicating about our feelings and being open and honest with each other. And (2) we speak good, life-giving words over each other. I was honest with him about how I was feeling.

When I was feeling self-conscious, I told him. Usually, he would start building me up and letting me know I didn't need to be self-conscious. Which leads to speaking good things over each other in the form of compliments. And this comes not only in the bedroom but in our day-to-day life. Whether we are at home or at the store, or wherever we may be, it's not uncommon for us to make little compliments to each other: "You're so good looking" or "You look really nice today". "You're awesome, I'm so glad that I'm married to you, You're the best" etc. Making comments like that will restore confidence and emotional intimacy in each other.

On the other hand, maybe it isn't you. Maybe you want to have sex, but your husband is the one disconnecting. As I mentioned before, this struggle is not one-sided and it is hard on your husband, too. You now know one of his deep secrets and he may be vulnerable. He may be feeling ashamed, embarrassed, and frustrated about the situation. You need to talk things out. If he isn't wanting to have sex, figure out why.

I am not a psychologist or counselor, but I do know that sex changes things. It brings you together like nothing else can. It is an integral part of your marriage that cannot be ignored. When you know your husband has been viewing porn, it is easy to get angry and want to give him the cold shoulder of intimacy, but that will not solve the problem. Instead, take some time to talk things out with your partner. Then, reconnect.

JOHNNIE: Sex is something that draws the man back in. It's a God- given desire. Your husband's desire may be stronger than yours and you need to understand that it is there. You can use it to your advantage! When your wife turns you down, it makes it harder to say no to porn, because you know you can get online and it's always a yes.

We don't have enough sex—that's why he looks at pornography: TRALSE (Eh, a little bit of both)

Notes:

1. https://www.msn.com/en-us/lifestyle/marriage/the-8-most-common-reasons-for-divorce/ss-AA3gtcM

6.
Myths: Or..Is It Him?

In the previous chapter we explored a lot of the mindsets that may be directed toward yourself when processing your husband's addiction. While there are plenty of self-demeaning thoughts that need to be analyzed, there is another category of thinking—It's all his fault!

#4 Clearly, he isn't a changed person.

I am glad people can't read my thoughts, aren't you? There are days when I feel like I have to "take my thoughts captive" more than I would like. Chances are, you are probably glad that people can't read your thoughts, either. Unfortunately, most people tend to elevate themselves over other people. And that's not right. We may be tricked into thinking that if we struggle less or do something better, then somehow, we are a better person. Turns out, people are people. They have intrinsic value just because they are a person. Some would say that Christians are the worst at this type of thinking. Many people who are in or who have encountered church life would say they felt judged by other Christians. Deep down, I think a lot of those judgments come from good intentions, they just have misplaced outlets and motives.

It is easy to think that a real Christian wouldn't get involved in sin. I know I had those same thoughts in dealing with Johnnie and his porn addiction. I thought he was Christian, I thought he was different! He was supposed to be a changed person! I relayed the story of what happened to Johnnie in Bolivia in 2005 in chapter 1. And I've thought about that story many times. It still amazes me that he understood his father in English when his father was speaking in Spanish. The events of the entire evening Johnnie later wrote down and finalized it by a sketch of a rope coming off his wrist and falling into God's glory. That evening was a turning point for Johnnie. Whether that night was the night he was saved or if it was an act of sanctification, I'm not sure. Either way, he changed that night, just as his father said. So, if God did such a great work in him, then why did he still struggle with porn? Where was the instantaneous deliverance? Pornography was different from that point on. It was still something he struggled with, but he was more determined than ever that it was a sinful habit and he needed to stop. But deliverance wasn't immediate.

When your spouse continues to struggle, it can be easy to doubt his commitment to you and even His commitment to Jesus. As a Christian, you are supposed to be changed and shouldn't have addictions. So, what happens when an addiction continues to linger? One thing I had to learn is that just because change doesn't happen immediately, doesn't mean that change isn't happening at all. Being saved doesn't mean that sin will lose all its allure. Anyone will tell you that sin is fun...for a season.

Craig Groeschel, who pastors one of the largest churches in America, has referenced many times in his sermons about sin, "If it isn't fun, you probably didn't do it right." Obviously, he wasn't advocating sinning, but rather stating that sin is alluring and that just because you are saved, it doesn't mean it stops being alluring. I don't think you need much convincing on this point. You may deal with it in a different way than your husband, but I know there are sinful things that still look alluring. Whether it's the attention you may get from sharing some gossip or something bigger, sin will look attractive.

There is so much to learn from Pap, my WWII veteran grandfather I mentioned previously. Another story he told me was regarding his conversion to Christianity. Pap was not a Christian when he was in the war. Well into his 90s, I saw him in tears of thankfulness, recounting the fact that while he did not know the Lord, yet the Lord kept him safe. As a child growing up in the 1920s and then going off to war, he was a smoker. In fact, we have a wartime picture of him sitting outside in France, propped up near a tree, smoking a cigarette. He continued his smoking habit even when he returned home from the war. He became a Christian within a couple years of returning from the war. The night he was saved, he had a pack of cigarettes in his shirt pocket. After he accepted the Lord, he never had another desire to smoke a cigarette. On top of that, he had no idea where the pack in his shirt even went. He never recalled throwing it away or getting rid of it—it was just gone.

Not everyone has that type of conversion story. You may get saved, but still struggle at times. Just because your struggle isn't porn doesn't mean that it is any different. Just as you may struggle, your husband struggles as well. The moment I was saved, I was a changed person. As the Bible says in 2 Corinthians 5:17, I was a new creation or creature, but that doesn't mean I did everything perfectly. Yes, I was convicted of my sin. But the older I've gotten, the more I've realized that God is still convicting me of certain things. I know I gossiped when I was younger, but I don't remember feeling convicted about it until later in life. It doesn't make it excusable, but it does show that our journey to be more like God is a process. He doesn't convict us of everything the moment we get saved. That would be discouraging! When you keep following the Lord and trusting Him and spending time with Him, He will continue to reveal those things to you.

When it comes to porn, your husband probably knows that viewing porn is wrong. But just because he is still struggling with it, doesn't mean that he isn't a changed person. Porn addictions, like any addictions, can have spiritual, physical, and emotional roots. It's hard to change all of those at once. Don't give up, and keep looking for progress, even if it is small. Yes, it's important that he is walking with the Lord, has a disciplined mind, and has the tools to help him break free from the addiction. But for now, keep praying for your spouse, encouraging your spouse, and knowing that as long as he is pursuing God, He will lead him on the right path. It may not be on your timetable, but it will happen. I love what Philippians says in chapter 1 verse 6 NLT: "And I am certain that God, who began the good work within you, will continue his work until it is finally finished on the day when Christ Jesus returns." Don't lose hope.

Clearly, he isn't a changed person: FALSE

My husband is a Christian, and I hope your spouse is too. I know that may not be the case, though. If your husband is not saved, be praying fervently for Him to be saved. Pray that God will draw Him to Jesus. If you go to church and he doesn't, try inviting him to go with you, or talk about a scenario in which he would be willing to come, as some people have different preferences in the type of church they attend. People can overcome addictions without being saved, but being a Christian makes all the difference.

#5 Porn is a self-medicating behavior.

In my discussions with Johnnie, one thing I found to be surprising was some of the other intentions of turning to pornography. As with many people, Johnnie was shown pornographic images at such a young age that it was a part of his life for years. He wasn't thinking about the physical and emotional intimacy with his wife when this addiction began to take root. As it progressed through high school and into college, he explained that it became a form of self-medication. The stressful times of high school and college and sometimes even the lack of control that day-to-day life threw his way, would cause him to turn to porn as an outlet.

With the changes in technology we find ourselves encountering and with the way the porn industry has grown, whatever men want to see, they can find. They can control it. No matter what, these women always "want" the viewer. Men don't have to worry about anyone else's feelings or emotions, and they don't have to warm up their partner, either. The viewer just gets the arousal and pleasure they want, when and how they want it.

I find this interesting because it seems like porn consumption isn't completely based on sexual drive, but rather trying to process other stressors. Instead of turning to other coping mechanisms, your spouse may turn to porn. Johnnie and I have listened to many sermons over the years, and one thing that has been mentioned many times is that temptation usually comes when people are weak. Not just a porn temptation, but any temptation to lead you away tends to strike when you are frustrated, stressed, tired, or hungry, that's when your guard is down and you are looking for something to meet your needs.

Satan and his adversaries are not new at this, they know when we are at our weakest and our self-control is low. It is during those times that the enemy attacks. In those times of attack, instead of making wise decisions, a compromise is made. For some, it may mean they compromise and eat a cream-filled doughnut instead of making a healthy choice for food. For your spouse, they may cave to the temptation of pornography instead of making a healthy decision.

Not to sound like a broken record, but pornography is always wrong, but remember you don't control your husband's choices. It's hard to see him make poor decisions, especially when they affect the family the way pornography does, but you cannot control him. There are times when there are other factors encouraging him to go down the road of lustful thoughts. Once again, it is never right, but having healthy communication about what is going on in life can help mitigate these things. If better coping mechanisms need to be in place, then discuss those things so his daily stress can be handled better and the outlet can be a healthy one.

He's doing this to self-medicate: Possibly TRUE

#6 If he really loved me, he would stop, right?

By far, this is the hardest question to answer. It's a scary question to explore and it can turn your husband into your enemy very quickly. At some point during my marriage, I've had to ask and answer each of these questions we have covered. Whenever this question would arise—and it arose many times—I felt I was swift to tears in thinking my husband was intentionally hurting me. It's a logical, if-then statement. If he loves me then he will stop looking at porn. Thus, if he doesn't love me then he won't stop looking at porn. And with that thought, we dive into the mental trap, convincing ourselves that our husbands don't care enough to stop. Have you had this question?

I'm not going to pretend to have the answer for every marriage scenario. Not every marriage is like mine and Johnnie's. Some get along better, and some aren't getting along at all. Some of you reading are at your wit's end in your marriage because your spouse doesn't want to change, while others of you have a committed husband who greatly wishes to change but feels trapped. Eventually, this question made it out of my mouth and to Johnnie's ears. I'm not sure how many times, but especially as I began to write this book, we talked about these different questions more.

I knew Johnnie loved me; I knew he did. He has shown his love in many ways over the years. So, I knew there had to be some part of the equation I was missing. I was amazed by the answer he gave me when I mentioned this question. He informed me that in the moment of the deepest, strongest temptation, it never really occurred to him that he was hurting me. I looked at him and said, "WHAT?? How could you not realize your actions would hurt me?"

He went on to say that the thoughts he would have—much of which are the same despite the type of bondage you are in—are focused on how much he needed porn. The whole situation felt like it was downplayed. He said he felt blind to the consequences leading up to watching porn. The enemy would feed him thoughts about how he just needed to get it out of his system, then he would be fine. Thoughts that would try to convince him that watching porn isn't that big of a deal. If he did have thoughts about my feelings, they were drowned out by the desire and drive.

With that, he would give in. Immediately afterward, remorse would hit like a ton of bricks. Those voices that were so convincing to get him to engage suddenly switched to condemnation. Instead of making his day easier by giving in to the lustful thoughts, it just made his day worse. He didn't want to tell me because he knew it hurt me. Each time he tried to keep it from me. He was convinced this time was the last time. Which, of course, wasn't true either.

Needless to say, that was not the answer I expected him to give. It had nothing to do with his level of love for me, but rather with him being blinded by temptation. And blind to our enemy trying to get him to give in, yet again. Our enemy is crafty, isn't he?

My husband is one for analogies. He has a great way of relating what he is thinking and feeling to various things.

Usually, they are from movies or are related to cars. He put this struggle into words by referencing a children's movie, Madagascar. In one scene toward the end, Alex the lion is so driven by his desire for meat that even his friends—whom he loves—appear to be pieces of meat, ready for him to devour. Next thing he knows, he is about to tear into his best friend, thinking he was a piece of meat, not realizing who he was hurting. Suddenly you see Alex snap to reality and realize what was going on—he was hurting his best friend. He then barricaded himself away from his friends to ensure he wouldn't accidentally eat them.

Johnnie recognized the feelings that Alex the lion was experiencing were remarkably similar to how men struggle with porn. The desire and drive become so strong that you don't realize who you are hurting. Like in the movie, you want to isolate and insulate yourself because you feel helpless. He had times when he felt like a monster and felt like he couldn't do anything right. It became so severe that it was leading to suicidal thoughts. He had reached the point where he knew he was hurting me. He was frustrated that he wasn't seeing much change in being free. I wasn't handling it well at this point, either. I was putting a lot of pressure on him instead of communicating in a healthy way.

Because he couldn't fix it, he felt like a failure, and it magnified everything else that didn't seem perfect in life. He began to think, "Can I do anything right? All I can do is screw up." It's a dark road to travel. I remember the first time he told me he wanted to run the car into a tree, just to end it all. I started to panic, seeing as how we were at a busy intersection and he was driving. He assured me that he would never act on those feelings, but he knew it was important to tell me the thoughts he was having.

Thank you, pornography.

Luckily, that season was short. And while those thoughts have come back occasionally over the years, he always reached out to those he trusted for support and was honest with me about when he was having those thoughts. And I made sure, to the best of my ability, that I was handling them in a safe way, too.

To re-visit the initial statement, ("If he loved me, he would stop.") it then becomes unfair to apply that reasoning to how our husbands are behaving. Your relationship is not something that should be used as leverage. Your marriage relationship is the paramount interpersonal relationship, don't use it as a bargaining chip.

As you think through this statement, it sets you up to make your husband your enemy instead of your partner. For instance, you start to doubt his love and air this ultimatum, "If you love me, you will stop." Your husband then could become nervous and fearful around you because he doesn't want you to know what he has been up to. If you find out he hasn't quit, then you might be convinced he doesn't love you and possibly leave. So, the secrecy continues.

You and your husband are partners in this fight. This battle isn't "his" thing, it's an "us" thing. We fight this together. While it is personal to him, you don't leave him helpless. You are there as his helper! It is easy to go down the "if" road. If he doesn't quit... Don't even look down that road. Be committed to trying to understand his side of things and how you can help.

I don't want to sound like I'm trying to excuse your

husband's addiction. But it is of utmost importance that you understand more of what he is going through. For most of us, our husbands feel trapped. They want to get out, but it's hard to see how. When you realize he is struggling just as you are struggling, this becomes less of an interpersonal fight and more of a partnership to see the future change.

If he really loved me, he would stop: FALSE

Your marriage relationship is the paramount interpersonal relationship, don't use it as a bargaining chip.

6.5
Who Ya Gonna Call?

We know the truth about who we are in Christ, and we have been able to dispel some common myths that are out there regarding pornography addictions, but sometimes it is still helpful to get the perspective of someone else. Honestly, you may just want someone you can talk to. I don't blame you; I was in the same boat! Even though I had begun to work through a lot of the feelings and emotions that accompany an addiction, I just wanted someone to hear my thoughts and reassure me that everything was going to be okay.

Unfortunately, pornography addictions aren't talked about much. It seems like it is an issue the church knows exists, but they haven't said much about how to combat the issue, besides mentioning that men should have self-control. There are some specialized small groups at churches that try to tackle the issue for men, but not many of those exist, either. Even less than that is the support for their spouses. I know I didn't talk to anyone about Johnnie's addiction because I was embarrassed about what Johnnie was dealing with. Would they think it was my fault, too? And not just for myself, but even though Johnnie was fighting, I still didn't want people to label him as a pervert and begin to treat him differently.

Johnnie would mention the addiction he was struggling with to different people in the context of small groups, but still, the spousal support was nil. The only people I ever spoke to about it were my mother-in-law and sister-in-law. I felt comfortable going to them because they already knew what Johnnie was struggling with. On top of that, Johnnie's parents are family and marriage counselors, so I knew that while it was personal, they could still be objective and give me some wisdom that others may not have.

Who are you going to talk to? It may be a mother or sister or friend from church, and those are fine. Just remember this is a sensitive issue and you don't want someone blabbering about this when you aren't around. Most importantly, whomever you speak with, outside of a pastor or counselor, please keep this woman to woman. This is not the time to turn to a trusted male friend or colleague. Unfortunately, that is how many affairs get started. A woman gets connected emotionally with a guy who isn't her husband and begins to lean on and appreciate his emotional support more so than her own spouse. Whether it is only an emotional affair or one that leads to a physical one, we want to be safe in our conversations, not open the door for further indiscretions.

Don't forget there are Christian counselors out there to help couples deal with issues in their marriage. Counseling may be a route the two of you choose to go down. Not only can a counselor help with the addiction, but he or she can also help you in how you are processing your emotions.

Never forget that while we do have professional help

83

we can turn to, there is one who is the original counselor, the Holy Spirit. He is our counselor and help, our advocate, and the one who empowers us. Before you speak to anyone, whether friends, family, or a professional, your first stop is in prayer.

In Galatians 1:15-16, Paul is recounting his experience when the Lord appeared to him. He says that he didn't consult with anyone or ask anyone's advice; instead, he went to Arabia by himself. After a few years, he went and met with the other apostles. Paul could've consulted with people, but instead, he took time to be alone with the Lord. During this time, the Lord revealed many things to him.

Many times, we go to others in hopes that they can give us the words that we want and need to hear. And while they may offer wisdom, nothing can replace the wisdom, guidance, and healing the Holy Spirit brings. Long before you suspected anything about your husband's secret addiction to pornography; the Holy Spirit knew the thoughts and intents of his heart. While it saddens the Lord that this is happening in your marriage, He isn't surprised, and His authority hasn't changed. He alone can bring hope to a hopeless situation and make things work for good when only disaster seems impending.

7.

Is Porn Wrong?

If you have ever traveled to a country that uses a different currency, then you know how confusing it can be trying to determine the value of the money in your hand. For instance, you may trade in $200 US dollars for the equivalent in Dominican pesos, but the money given back to you doesn't quite seem to match the amount you traded in.

Throughout my life, I have done some traveling and most places I have visited do not use the US dollar. On one such trip, we were in the Dominican Republic looking for some little trinkets for our kids. We saw this cute little wooden airplane that we knew our older son would love. The price? $500. Now, if we didn't understand the value of what we had, we probably would have quickly passed over the airplane and found a nice magnet instead. But, because we understood what we had in our hands, we knew that $500 Dominican Pesos was about $10 in US currency. Knowing the value of something is especially important. When we were in the Dominican Republic, we knew the money we had was important, but we had to figure out its value.

Value…how things are valued has seen quite the change over time. We have belongings, but we look at most of those things as being replaceable. Relationships are replaceable, TVs are replaceable, even the newest phones will soon be replaced with a newer model. And to help pay for that newer model, we have the ever-present credit card offers encouraging us to buy now and pay later, usually with the tagline of, "You deserve it." We have turned into a culture and people who don't have to wait to get what we want. It doesn't matter if there is money in the bank or not, what matters is what "I" want. I deserve it, I need it, so I will go and get it now! The repercussions are not simply monetary, but that same mindset has impacted most areas of our lives, including sexuality, which is how this relates to pornography.

Recently, I had a comment on one of our YouTube videos in which the commenter said that there wasn't anything wrong with porn. In fact, he and his partner watch it together! He's not alone. There is a host of people who think there is nothing wrong with pornography. Have you heard similar things? Some may not understand why you are upset, citing the fact that your spouse isn't interacting with a real woman. I've heard it, too. This chapter is packed with information about the foundation and value of purity from a Biblical perspective, so rest assured, you aren't blowing this issue out of proportion, pornography is wrong.

Why this change of perspective, though? Why are people more accepting of this idea that porn is okay? I don't know about you, but I have noticed a substantial devaluing of marriage faithfulness, purity, and virginity in my own lifetime, and that's just since the late 80s! But the devaluation has been going on much longer than that. In the time of the Bible, a woman could be severely punished if she was not a virgin on her wedding night. In the 21st century, it is the complete opposite. My husband was told by co-workers before we were married that he better "try me out" first to make sure we were compatible in bed. That's a complete change! While I can't point to a specific event or time when things shifted, a quote by Damon Thompson sums it up, "Today's compromise is tomorrow's stronghold." As time has passed on, compromises have been made and generation after generation has made choices that have eventually led to a society that has lost the value of sex, virginity, purity, and marriage faithfulness.

The music industry saw the change in the 1950s and 60s with explicit material being included in songs. Exposure to sexually explicit material is happening earlier in the lives of people, and we are seeing more and more of the onslaught of sexual crimes. Pornography is at an all-time high. It's staggering to see how things have changed. Sadly, in our culture, knowing and understanding the value of sexuality and virginity is quickly being lost. I understand that virginity isn't the topic of this book, especially seeing as how if you are reading this book, you are probably married. However, to understand the value of purity and marriage faithfulness, we need to go back and understand virginity because ultimately these have the same root, and that is purity. While purity has one context before marriage, that being virginity, there is also a level of purity after you are married. And by that, I mean that you won't be comprising sexually in any way outside of the God-given bounds of marriage. Marriage faithfulness doesn't only start when you are initially married, but the foundation starts with how you value sex before you even begin to date.

I understand not everyone who is reading this book was a virgin when they were married. As we are talking about the value and importance of virginity, please don't feel condemned by an action that you cannot change. Or perhaps you didn't have a choice, you cannot change what happened, but you can change the future, and that is what this book is working toward. Having an appropriate understanding of this topic can greatly serve us as we are healing and greatly serve the next generation.

So what does the Bible say about porn, purity, and virginity? If you're looking for the verse that says, "Thou shalt not view pornography", well, you won't find it. In fact, you won't find the word "pornography" in the Bible at all, but the concept for the word is found. The Bible references sexual immorality from cover to cover. When the words "sexual immorality" are translated, we get one Greek word. The Greek word is porneia. (Sounds really close to the word pornography if you ask me!) The word porneia means the "selling off (surrendering) of sexual purity." When the Bible condemns sexual immorality, it is against what is being done to surrender your sexual purity, whether it be an adulterous relationship, premarital sex, or anything else outside the confines of what God has deemed to be an appropriate sexual relationship. As you know, the only sexual relationship that God explicitly blesses and approves of is that between a husband and his wife. Anything outside of that is sin.

While pornography didn't exist in the same context in Biblical days as it does now, there is clear Biblical evidence that pornography would fall under the realm of "sexual immorality." The Bible has plenty to say about marriage relationships, sex, and sexual immorality. In fact, sexuality is mentioned in both literal and metaphorical terms from Genesis to Revelation.

A Quick Trip Through the Bible

Before we look in-depth at a couple of passages, we're going to take a broad overview of what the Bible says about sex, purity, and sexual immorality. And some of these instances include where different men and women act sexually based on what they see. While they didn't have a computer screen, magazine, or phone, they still violated God's laws based on what they saw, and in each of those cases, something sexual was seen, and it led to big consequences.

As Genesis chapter 2 closes, we see Adam say that Eve is a part of him. A mandate is given that husbands are to leave their families to cling to their wives and they are to be united into one flesh. This is the first mention of sex we have in the Bible. As generations pass, matters on earth go from garden perfection to a level of corruption so bad it results in a worldwide flood. After this flood, only Noah and his family are left and they are tasked with populating the earth again. To make a long story short, even after the flood, mankind has never made the best decisions when it comes to sex and impurity. Just reading through Genesis, you will see many violations of the sexual purity ideals expected of God's people between a man and wife.

At the end of Genesis 9, there is an awkward scenario regarding Noah's son Ham seeing Noah naked. There is a bit of a debate as to whether Ham did something more than just see Noah's nakedness, but that's not the point I want to make here. He saw his father uncovered and instead of honoring his father and covering him, he told his brothers. Then his brothers, walking backward, covered their father. The result is that Noah's two older sons were blessed, but Ham's youngest son, Canaan, was cursed. Fast forward a few chapters in Genesis, and you read of Sodom, Gomorrah, and the cities on the plain that were notorious for their sexual sin.

You can't mention some of the sexual sins in the Bible without thinking about David in I Samuel. King David was supposed to be out to war, instead, he was at home. He walked out on his roof and saw Bathsheba. He didn't bounce his eyes and look at something else, but he continued to watch her. Instead of avoiding temptation, he kept looking, falling headlong into its trap. He acted on what he saw and thus became guilty of lust, it escalated to adultery, and culminated in murder. The consequence? The son of this union between David and Bathsheba died. There are many warnings in the Bible that warn its readers to avoid anything that will tempt them sexually—there are always consequences.

On the flip side, the Old Testament is riddled with stories, similes, and metaphors pointing toward the value of purity. There are stories of brothers killing another man for the honor of their sister who was raped. When the Ten Commandments are given in Exodus, we have the mandate to not commit adultery, and throughout Leviticus more specific laws regarding sexuality are given. In Deuteronomy, the rules for divorce are stated. There's an interesting passage that we will read momentarily about the consequences if a woman is found not to be a virgin on her wedding night. The sexually immoral were killed, in many cases. Psalm 101 mentions not putting any worthless or vile things in front of your eyes. In Proverbs, there are many warnings against prostitutes and adultery.

As you read through the major and minor prophets of the Old Testament, you see the nation of Israel being symbolically cast as the prostitute. The Bible compares the relationship that God has with His people to that of a man and wife. She was not loyal and pure to her covenant with God, but rather she compromised with other gods. He brings many complaints against the Israelites saying they have committed adultery. They promised in the covenant to follow God and only God, to be purely devoted to Him. However, they began to worship other gods and joined themselves to those entities instead of the one, true God. She is seen as one who walks out on her commitment to a loving God who is there to supply all her needs, and what is expected of her in return is to honor the covenant.

As the Bible transitions to the New Testament, the message doesn't change. Throughout the Gospels (Matthew, Mark, Luke, & John), we read about Jesus discussing sexual immorality, then there is the iconic story of the woman who was caught in the act of adultery, and it is also in the Gospels where Jesus lays out the rules for divorce. The remainder of the New Testament has different authors admonishing their readers to flee lust (2 Timothy 2:22), as well as what a Biblical marriage should look like (Ephesians 5). Even the book of Revelation references those who are pure and those who are sexually immoral.

From that short synopsis, we can see that sexual purity, before and during marriage is of great importance. We can also see the seriousness that God takes with being bound to anything other than that for which you were created.

Going Deeper

Let's take this topic a bit deeper and explore some concepts and passages of scripture that will continue to shed light on what the Bible has to say about pornography.

Marriage is a covenant, and a covenant is a promise.

When you married your spouse, you made a covenant together. The covenant or promise is made at the wedding ceremony during the recitation of the vows. Now, take yourself back to the 2nd grade version of yourself, how did you seal a promise? Pinky promise? Handshake? Spit handshake? I was usually a pinky-promise kind of person. No worries, I grew out of that before our wedding ceremony. I mention that because it shows we can all identify with sealing a promise with an action. The Bible is no different. Throughout the Bible, as God made different covenants with his people, there was bloodshed. Bloodshed was always the way God sealed a promise.

First, we read of the old covenant, which is the law that we find in the Old Testament. The New Testament is called the New Testament because it details the new covenant or the new promise that God was establishing with His people and the people of the world. Jesus sealed this new covenant with his blood when He died on the cross. God didn't intend just to make a promise to us, but rather to make a blood covenant—a promise that can't be broken. Some carry that same covenant standard to the marriage bed. The following is controversial, and I mention it to show you only the seriousness of the marriage covenant, I am not necessarily saluting it as doctrine.

I find it interesting that in Deuteronomy 22 we have an instance where a man and wife are married and after their wedding night, he claims he discovers that she is not a virgin. At this point, it is up to the bride's parents to show the garment stained with blood from their daughter's wedding night. It was a common practice to keep the proof of her virginity, as many women bleed after their first sexual encounter. The punishment was dependent upon whether the evidence could be supplied. From this, many have proposed marriage as a blood covenant;

a promise that is sealed with bloodshed, the same way that God made His covenant with us—a covenant that wasn't meant to be broken. Whether it is a blood covenant or not we may never fully know, but the importance shouldn't be lost. Marriage is to be entered into with purity, and with a commitment to never leave your spouse, just as God wouldn't walk out on the promises He made to us.

In hermeneutics (which is a big word meaning the study/interpretation of the Bible), there is a principle called the Law of First Mentions. It simply means that when you are studying a Biblical topic, you need to go back to the first time the word or concept was mentioned in Scripture to get the purest meaning of the topic. Abiding by this law, let's look again at the first time the concept of sex is discussed in the Bible. It takes us back to Genesis 2:23-25 ESV: "Then the man said, "This at last is bone of my bones and flesh of my flesh; she shall be called Woman, because she was taken out of Man." Therefore a man shall leave his father and his mother and hold fast to his wife, and they shall become one flesh. And the man and his wife were both naked and were not ashamed."" One Hebrew Lexicon describes the word for "holding fast or cleaving" to mean they were glued. You are to leave your mother and father and be glued to your spouse. This glue isn't the little glue sticks you use in kindergarten, and it's not a marriage ceremony sealed with a pinky promise, either. So, what is the glue that binds a couple together? What is the sealing of the marriage covenant promise?

It's sex. Sex connects. You are to be one with your spouse. That is why sex is referred to as the consummation of marriage; it makes the marriage covenant complete. In fact, if you don't have sex after you are married, it can nullify the marriage. Without sex, the marriage is incomplete. Sex is the act that binds couples together, it is the glue that takes us from two separate beings to one flesh.

The verse from Genesis we just read isn't the only passage that mentions this, either. In 1 Corinthians 6:16 ESV it says, "Or do you not know that he who is joined to a prostitute becomes one body with her? For, as it is written, "The two will become one flesh." Once again, if you look at the meaning of the Greek words used in this text, it means "to glue or cement". It is not a simple marriage ceremony that makes you "glued" together, but rather having sex. Sex is the bond of marriage. That's why purity matters. Virginity matters because if you are having sex with others, you are gluing yourself to them. You are binding yourself to them. While time may pass, you will always have that connection. And just like the Israelites were meant to be bound only to the true God, you are meant to be bound to your spouse only.

I realize you're reading this book because your spouse had the indiscretion, not you, but it's still good information to help lay a foundation for the Biblical case against any impurity in the marriage bed. Unfortunately, many give up not only their physical virginity, but their marriage purity because they want immediate pleasure. They aren't worried about their decision to be bound to someone else. They just want to fulfill the desires they have, no matter the consequences. It's the same concept we see in many advertisements: "Buy now, pay later!" Experience your desires now—pay for them later. To some, the following will be a trivial comparison; however, it does put a picture in your head as to what it can mean to be bound to something when it wasn't a good decision.

I had only known Johnnie for a couple months when he

excitedly walked me and a few friends outside to show us his new car. As we were walking through the parking lot, Johnnie announced, "Here she is!" I thought he was joking. This was not a new car. We were looking at a 1992 Geo Storm hatchback—and we were in the fall of 2006. This fourteen-year-old car had clearly seen better days. Even if it was in perfect condition, it looked like a spaceship and the grill made it appear as if the car was smiling. (Go ahead, take a moment and look up a picture of this car. I'll wait.) I almost laughed at the joke, but then I realized he was serious. This was his new car. To think of someone having a "new" car that was 14 years old and falling apart, I was not impressed.

Over the year—that's right, one year—that it ran, I grew to love that little smiling spaceship car. After it went the way of the junkyard, Johnnie brought over his next "new" car. I was prepared this time, or so I thought. This time he pulled up in a 1987 Pontiac Bonneville, a grandma's special! Low miles, comfortable seats, and older than I was. He drove "Bonny" from that point in our relationship to several years into our marriage. Eventually, we convinced ourselves that the monthly maintenance wasn't worth it, and a new car would be much easier.

We wanted something new and reliable, so we bought ourselves a much newer car, and with it, came our first car loan. We didn't want to wait and save our money for the car we really wanted. We just wanted something different, something newer and we wanted it now. We were so excited about the car that the loan didn't seem that big of a deal at the time. We would have rather have what we wanted at that moment and pay more be-cause of the loan and be in debt, rather than wait and save our money. We were so excited about our new car…and then the first payment hit. Month after month, payment after payment.

We were joined by contract to that car. The car lost its excitement because every month we were bound by the payment. We couldn't undo that decision. The contract was signed, and we were committed. Our only option was to pay it off.

Before long, we sold it, paid off our loan, and purchased something much cheaper that we wouldn't have to make monthly payments on. I realize our society looks at debt as a normal thing now. For us, debt was not okay, and it was not something we wanted to get trapped by. But we did, because it goes back to those credit card offers and other advertisements of, "Buy now, pay later! You deserve it." As it turns out, we didn't deserve it; we regretted it. Unlike video games, you can't just restart the game. The decisions you make are now yours to deal with.

Now think of how this applies to sexuality. Think about the messages that are bombarding men, women, and teenagers every day. It might not be said, but it's understood. Enjoy your one-night stands, and non-committed sexual relationships, enjoy your pornography now, but you'll pay for it later. You deserve to feel pleasure now, why wait? Yes, you'll have to pay for it, but it will be later. Live for the now, it's easier this way!

In Matthew 5:28, Jesus tells us that if a man looks at a woman lustfully, he has already committed adultery with her in his heart. When one is involved in pornography, a few things are happening. First, there is lust. The dictionary defines lust as having a "very strong sexual desire." As the images are being viewed and the desire arises, unfortunately, it isn't for you, his wife. It's for whoever is in the image. Here's the first infraction. While there isn't another person there physically engaging with him, his mental actions are still sinful.

The mental attraction is one part; however, an action

usually follows. What would normally bind you to your spouse, instead is an empty action. It binds you further to the obsession, the lust, and the secrecy. It becomes an illegitimate union. Many have asked the question, "Is it the masturbation that is wrong, or is just the lustful thoughts?" You will find many different answers to this question, but I believe this is probably one of the most complete answers: "If done with absolutely no lust, immoral thoughts, or pornography, with full assurance that it is good and right, with thanks given to God for the pleasure it brings (1 Corinthians 10:30), is it still a sin to masturbate? The most we can say is maybe not. However, we have serious doubts whether this scenario ever truly exists." [1] Unfortunately, there is no good that comes from viewing porn, and there is no Biblical evidence that it is a moral action. Instead, it's the complete opposite.

While sexual immorality is always wrong and pornography is always wrong, I have compassion for those who are dealing with this addiction. They were sold a bill of lies, and now they have to figure out how they are going to pay for it and get out of this addiction. When we do something the world's way, we must pay for it. Sometimes you pay for it monetarily, other times there are different physical consequences. When we choose to bind ourselves to things outside of the will of God, it will affect us. But when we do things God's way and stay pure, we reap God's rewards.

Notes:

1. https://www.gotquestions.org/masturbation-sin.html

8.
Porn Statistics

I t may seem counter-intuitive that we need to define what pornography is, but we each have different ideas of what it can be. So, I want to add a little clarification on the point. When I think of pornography, I define it as images or videos portraying sexually elicit or suggestive material.

Believe it or not, there are debates over the definition of pornography. We know in general terms what it is, however, different people struggle in different ways. What is sexually suggestive to one person, may not be to another. As I am taking you through my and Johnnie's story, when I say he has struggled with pornography, it has ranged in frequency and use. There was a time when he was a frequent viewer. Then, there were times when he would go months without looking. It varied. As time went on, the frequency was less and less.

The medium also changed. Much of the time, initially, he was visiting pornography sites, it later changed to being able to see different suggestive images that can be innocently found.

With your spouse, it may be something similar. The frequency may change, depending on the circumstances, and the sites or medium he uses to access pictures or videos may change as well. But one thing doesn't change, and that is the seriousness of this issue. While we need to celebrate small gains in the area of overcoming this major hurdle, it is still an issue whether it is being viewed once an hour or once a year.

While statistics don't mean everything, they are a good indicator of where problems are and very enlightening in understanding certain situations. In our journey to process our emotions, understand our spouse's struggle, and ultimately reveal the truth, we need to know the industry that our husbands are fighting against. This information will help you arm yourself with the knowledge that you are not alone in combating this giant. Let's start out with a discouraging quote from Paul Fishbein, Founder of Adult View News[1]:

Porn doesn't have a demographic—it goes across all demographics.

Uplifting, right? Why is that quote true? Well, because sexuality affects everyone. Sexual desire is something that we all experience. God created it, and it is powerful. It's been around since the beginning! In fact, some refer to prostitution as the world's oldest profession. Forbes did an article related to this subject saying that the art of selling is actually the world's oldest profession—going all the way back to when the snake "sold" the apple (or whatever piece of fruit it was) to Eve in the Garden of Eden.[2]

Forbes may have a point. When it comes to sexual compromise, it does go back to the idea of selling something. If you remember earlier when we defined "porneia" it was linked to the selling or surrendering of one's sexual purity. Of course, there are times when physical money does change hands, but it is more than that. It's the selling of a lie or a counterfeit. Everything about pornography is a lie. It is staged and those involved are actors. They are selling this lie that intimacy with your spouse is going to be hyper-sexualized.

JOHNNIE: When you are watching these women, they are trying to pull you in. Because of this, I felt trained to expect sex to be ultra-sexy and serious. But remember, these men and women are actors. And just like we know that life in movies is not real, so it is with porn. It doesn't show a realistic expectation of what sex is actually like.

Porn is selling the idea that meeting your sexual needs, desires, and fantasies—despite whom they are with—will mean ultimate fulfillment; and that statement is simply not true. While sex is a powerful thing, it is not the sole purpose of existence. We are believing a lie if we think that our sexual fulfillment is the be-all and end-all. Porn is no different. It's easy to think, "Well, he has sexual needs, and this is an outlet for him." Or "He doesn't do it all that time, so it's not that big of a deal." It is an addiction, yes, but it is also a counterfeit. Porn is not meant to fulfill sexual needs.

Updated porn statistics, like divorce statistics, can be tricky to find. These numbers are a few years old, but still paint a gruesome picture of what we are encountering today. Unfortunately, these numbers aren't getting better. In fact, from the time of some of these statistics, porn has become more available across more devices, and to younger ages. Here are some notable statistics regarding the pornography industry[3]:

- Every second 28,258 users are watching pornography on the internet.
- Every second $3,075.64 is being spent on pornography on the internet.
- Every second 372 people are typing the word "adult" into search engines.
- 40 million American people regularly visit porn sites.
- 35% of all internet downloads are related to pornography.
- 25% of all search engine queries are related to pornography, or about 68 million search queries a day.
- One-third of porn viewers are women.
- Search engines get 116,000 queries every day related to child pornography.
- 34% of internet users have experienced unwanted exposure to pornographic content through ads, pop up ads, misdirected links, or emails.
- 2.5 billion emails sent or received every day contain porn.
- Every 39 minutes a new pornography video is being created in the United States.
- According to National Coalition for the Protection of Children & Families, 2010, 47% of families in the United States reported that pornography is a problem in their home.
- Pornography use increases the marital infidelity rate by more than 300%

- 68% of divorce cases involve one party meeting a new paramour over the internet while 56% involve one party having an "obsessive interest" in pornographic websites.

And these:

- 90% of American young men 18 and younger have been exposed to porn.
- The average age of first exposure is between 8-11 years old.[4]
- Porn sites receive more regular traffic than Netflix, Amazon, & Twitter combined each month.[5]
- Porn is a global, estimated $97 billion industry, with about $12 billion of that coming from the U.S.[6]
- In 2016 alone, more than 4,599,000,000 hours of porn were consumed on the world's largest porn site.[7]
- Eleven pornography sites are among the world's top 300 most popular Internet sites. The most popular such site, at number 18, outranks the likes of eBay, MSN, and Netflix.[8]
- 64% of young people, ages 13–24, actively seek out pornography weekly or more often.[9]

I could go on and on listing the statistics of porn and its widespread use. However, they aren't all useful to what we are discussing, as you already know that pornography is a problem. The aforementioned statistics give a grim picture. While the chances of pornography being eradicated on a worldwide scale are minuscule, as the women of our families, we need to do what we can to eradicate it from our homes.

With statistics as concerning as those mentioned above, it is no surprise that so many are struggling with an addiction. Which begs the question, what is a pornography addiction? How does someone go so quickly from a view to an addiction? I understand that any amount of pornography consumption is hurtful and sinful, as it is a violation of mental purity in marriage. But it can be helpful to understand what your spouse could possibly be going through, so I wanted to offer some brief information on addictions and brains. Obviously, I am not an expert in the field of addictions, but my armchair research has taught me much about what is going on neurologically in the mind of an addict.

Some men only look at porn occasionally. They wouldn't consider themselves addicted, but the door to this temptation has been opened and has been walked through. Other men may have a much higher consumption rate and are considered as one who has an addiction. Some may consume daily or multiple times a day, while others may be less. If you read scholarly articles written about addictions, particularly pornography addictions, you will find different opinions on the matter as to its morality. While society may have different opinions on the matter, we have already discussed the standards of purity the Bible places on men and women of faith.

It is interesting to read about the effects pornography has on the brain. Harvard Medical School published an article on addictions that I am going to summarize in this section. I'll include the link in the footnotes if you would like to read it in its entirety. This article opens by explaining how the word "addiction" is taken from a Latin term meaning "enslaved by" or "bound to". It explains how addictions influence the brain in three ways: craving the object of the addiction, loss of control over its use, and continuing involvement despite adverse consequences.

According to the scientific community, an addiction is categorized as a disease because of how it can hijack the brain. At this point, when I read the article, I was surprised to read it was considered a disease. I had heard similar things over the years, but I wasn't aware there was a resolute decision. Please understand, though, that even though an addiction may be considered a disease by some standards, it isn't without personal responsibility. This article is not saying that your husband just happened to contract a pornography disease. That's absurd. However, part of the technical definition of a disease is "a condition that impairs normal functioning." And with that, we proceed with the article.

Here's what happens in the brain that can lead to an addiction. First, some type of pleasure is experienced. Whenever the brain experiences any type of pleasure, whether related to the topic at hand or something else entirely, it releases dopamine. "The likelihood that the use of a drug or participation in a rewarding activity will lead to addiction is directly linked to the speed with which it promotes a dopamine release, the intensity of that release, and the reliability of that release."

Dopamine interacts with other neurotransmitters, and they affect the reward circuit in the brain. This reward circuit involves things like memory, motivation, and pleasure. Addictive behaviors overload this circuit. Repeated exposure causes the nerve cells to interpret the feelings as liking them and wanting them. "Addictive... behaviors provide a shortcut, flooding the brain with dopamine and other neurotransmitters." Over time, it takes more dopamine to experience the same type of "high" because the brain has begun to adapt to increased levels of dopamine. Interestingly enough, this area of the brain can help influence how things are learned and remembered when someone encounters "environmental cues" that are common when experiencing the addiction. The brain remembers those things and the compulsion to take part in the activity happens.

This explanation is one reason why people of all different addiction types have the possibility of relapsing even after a long period of resisting those urges. A person encounters something in their day-to-day life that is related to when the addiction would happen, and this memory has already conditioned the brain on what to expect, thus creating the craving.[10]

I understand the previous paragraph may sound like we're revisiting biology class and because of the risk of zoning out, you may not want to revisit that. To put it more simply, I've heard others explain the addictive process as being compared to a path in the woods:

Imagine the brain as the wilderness and throughout this wilderness, there are different pathways called neuronal pathways. A new path is started in the brain when you are learning a new skill, or what can eventually become an addiction. Over time, as the path gets worn, it becomes easier and easier to go down and more permanent. This process is great when you are learning a new skill; however, when someone is looking at pornographic image after image, they are creating well-worn pathways in the brain, and the brain is remembering the environmental cues that were around when all the "feel good" chemicals were released. The good news is that these pathways can be reversed. Just as a path worn in the woods will be overgrown when there isn't consistent foot traffic, so those neuronal pathways can change when a "porn pathway is not reinforced."[11]

Understanding how the brain works when facing an addiction can help give you some perspective as to what your spouse is going through. As I just mentioned, the brain remembers the environmental cues during porn exposure, whether it's people, feelings, smells, etc. Johnnie has been so open with me over the years about what he has experienced, and his openness has helped me gain a greater understanding.

Years ago, we were watching a popular show together. I had seen more episodes than he had, but occasionally he would watch them with me. During one of these episodes, he informed me one of the main characters had gotten his start in porn videos. Johnnie went on to tell me that every time he sees this actor, he can't help but remember the industry that gave this actor his start. Thus, it was an environmental cue.

Now, that doesn't mean Johnnie was being tempted, but those were the image memories associated with this particular actor. Over the years, Johnnie has mentioned the same observation about numerous actors in the entertainment we have watched. Some male, some female, and every time unexpected, as the shows we watch are clean. Usually, as soon as that realization is mentioned, there is an immediate change to watch something different. I don't want Johnnie to struggle mentally just because we don't want to turn off the show. At the same time, I don't want to do anything that would reinforce any old pathways that are well on their way to disappearing.

Viewing an addiction as a pathway worn in the woods is a great mental picture. It doesn't guarantee that your spouse is going to be slow to change, but it can give you a picture of the damage that has been done up to this point. Because those pathways are well-worn, when temptation arises, it is quite easy for the brain to make those connections it has made numerous times in the past. It is difficult for the brain to experience those environmental cues and then take a different path.

But please know, it can happen. It will happen. Johnnie wasn't immediately delivered from his porn addiction, but over time things changed. There are others, and I've known them, whom God has miraculously delivered instantaneously. Don't be discouraged if your spouse has a relapse, but rather take hope that your spouse will change, and one day that well-worn pathway will be unrecognizable.

In closing this section, I know you are in pain, and I know you are probably discouraged; but don't lose hope. You may not be to the point where you are starting to recover yet. I hope that forgiving your husband and understanding more of his side of the struggle has helped you come to grips with the root of this addiction. Restoration will come. Joy will come. But in the waiting, we have hope. We always have hope. Don't give up, even when the addiction seems like it is getting worse, or even if your husband doesn't care to quit—don't give up. The impossible can happen. Your marriage can be restored and renewed. Trust can be rebuilt, and your pain can be healed.

Notes:

1. https://www.covenanteyes.com/2013/02/19/pornog-

raphy-statistics/

2. https://www.forbes.com/sites/jimblasin-game/2015/08/14/the-oldest-profession-is-not-what-youthink #734d303ded6d

3. https://www.forbes.com/sites/jimblasin-game/2015/08/14/the-oldest-profession-is-not-what-you-think/#734d303ded6d

4. http://thenovusproject.org/resource-hub/parents

5. http://www.huffingtonpost.com/2013/05/03/inter net-porn-stats_n_3187682.html

6. http://www.nbcnews.com/business/business-news/things-are-looking-americas-porn-industry-n289431

7. https://fightthenewdrug.org/most-popular-porn-genre-search-of-2016/

8. https://www.similarweb.com/blog/new-website-rank-ing

9. https://fightthenewdrug.org/media/64-of-young-peo-ple-2/

10. https://www.health.harvard.edu/newsletter_article/how-addiction-hijacks-the-brain

11. https://fightthenewdrug.org/how-porn-changes-the-brain/

9.
Communication: Part 1

Pap, my WWII grandfather who I told you about earlier, was born in 1924, so he saw technology change a lot. During one of our many conversations, I asked him, "What has been the most surprising technological advancement during your lifetime?" My mind raced as I anticipated his answer. Could it be air conditioning or heating? Perhaps it was seeing and installing indoor plumbing in homes! Or maybe it was computers or credit and debit cards.

It was none of these. His answer was the telephone. He went on to tell me of war stories in which they had walkie-talkies that were so unreliable, you couldn't hear someone thirty feet away. On top of that, to use these walkie-talkies you had to wear a cumbersome backpack. He said that he has been able to see the transition from those primitive communication devices to cell phones, computers, and now features like video calls. Which, I will add, up until his death in 2021 at the age of 97, he did remarkably well receiving video calls! Pap said the advancements have been remarkable.

Speaking of Pap, the war story he would tell the most is when he was left behind by his unit. His company of men had just taken out a German machine gun nest, and the Germans that were in the area had retreated. A few American soldiers stayed in the machine gun nest and Pap and another soldier had advanced up a hill and set up an outpost. Shortly thereafter, the Germans started firing artillery at them. The men in the machine gun nest went and got the other soldier that had set up the outpost, but they didn't make it up to my grandfather to inform him their unit was now falling back. So, Pap was left at an advanced position, all alone.

When the firing started, my grandfather dug a small foxhole and just sat there and read a book he had in his pack. He said he was there for about 3 hours. Eventually, his sergeant found him and was relieved to see him alive because they thought he had been killed. Pap told his sergeant what happened, and how he just dug in and relaxed. In retrospect, Pap told us that he was more scared after the fact when he realized how dangerous the situation was. The entire time he was dug in, he figured his unit was all around him, but they weren't. He thought he had backup and the support of the other men in his unit, but he was left alone, defenseless.

Can you imagine being on a battlefield in Europe and being all alone? You have no way to communicate with your unit. You can't text them, no Snap Chat, no FaceTime, and certainly no GPS. I know all of us would agree that the aforementioned scenario would be awful. We think those things because we know how vital communication is during life-and-death situations. As Pap saw firsthand, the stakes are high! If the US Army and their Allied forces were defeated, there would've been monumental repercussions.

Let's take that same knowledge of communication and look at your marriage in light of a porn addiction. Communication is vital. You can't go without it. You can't depend on unreliable means of communication and hope you make it through. This is the time to over-communicate. This is the time to make sure you know exactly who is going where and doing what. You are in a battle for your marriage. If you are defeated, there are repercussions!

There are few things more important in a marriage than communication. What is communication? Have you thought about that before? It seems like a simple question and something that is assumed, but there is a lot more that goes into communication than one may know.

I taught high school English for a couple of years before having a family, and one unit I added in every year was on communication and public speaking. I would ask my students the same question: What is communication? Many times, students would say that communication is whatever you are saying. However, that is incorrect. Communication is any message you are sending, whether it be with your words or with your actions. It is the process of sending, receiving, and understanding a message. As we all know, there is also non-verbal communication. If you have been married for any length of time, you will have had those times with your spouse when you exchange a look, and no words need to be said. You know exactly what is being communicated.

In 2005, the movie Hitch came to theaters. In the opening scenes, Will Smith talks about communication and mentions some statistics about nonverbal communication, including saying that most of what you are communicating, isn't coming from your mouth.[1] Meaning, you have words you are saying, but also included in that message is your posture, your tone of voice, the look on your face, etc. Unfortunately, many times those non-verbal messages carry more weight than the words you say. A quick internet search will prove to you that effective communication is not only a vital part of a marriage, but it is also a factor that is failing to take place in a lot of marriages.

Communicating about the weather or your weekend plans is usually a painless conversation. However, communicating about your spouse's porn addiction can be tricky. As a woman who may be feeling victimized, it is easy to be defensive, frustrated, and saddened. Your spouse is experiencing his own emotions during this conversation, and he may be feeling ashamed, frustrated, and mad. You both may be joined by the common emotion of feeling somewhat insecure. As his wife, it is easy to wonder if he is going to leave you for what he is seeing online. And the men may be having thoughts of, "Is she going to leave me because I can't control myself?"

During the writing of this book, Johnnie had relapses. He would do fine for a period of time, then slip up. So, please know that throughout this writing process, we have still been in the trenches fighting temptation, communicating, forgiving, and being reconciled. In my late teen years, it would sometimes frustrate me to read books about being single and waiting for Mr. Right that were written by women who were already married. While I appreciated their content, and I found it helpful, I also wanted to read books from women who were still on that journey. It's easy to look back and see the lessons learned, but where were the women who were still in the thick of it? I wanted to know how I could thrive in the process. Well, I am that person, and we are that couple. We are still in this battle. I still get frustrated and saddened by Johnnie's confessions. But I have not and will not lose hope.

I am confident by the time this book goes to print and is in your hands, we will have closed the door on this issue, but we aren't quite there yet—we are so close, and Johnnie has come such a long way. Until then, I will choose to remain joyful despite the battle we are in and choose to show my spouse unconditional love, just as Jesus did for us and just as Hosea did for Gomer. I realize you may not know who Hosea and Gomer are yet, but you will know soon! There is an interesting correlation between their story and what we are talking about.

By this time, I'm assuming that you and your spouse have had some time to talk about the issue at hand. Hopefully, you have taken the opportunity to express your forgiveness and support for your spouse. If you haven't, that is the first thing to talk about. You need to make sure your spouse knows that you are choosing not to hold this against him and that he has your support for recovery. To ensure we are all on the same page, when I say let your husband know that you are supporting him, it is support for him to recover from this addiction. You are supporting him in the midst of this addiction, but not supporting him to continue in his sinful, hurtful behavior. One of the best ways for you to show your support is your expression of being willing to help. And how you help really comes into play when we discuss accountability in a future chapter.

After your spouse knows that he has your support, the two of you need to talk about some feelings, emotions, and motivations involved in this. While this conversation may not feel natural to talk about, be calm and considerate. This conversation shouldn't be a replay of an interrogation scene from a crime show. It is not a time for you to press your spouse for any specific details about what was viewed. The times my husband has slipped up, we always talk about it afterward. He will tell me things like what device was used, when it happened, and occasionally the website or source that was viewed. That's it. There is no, "What was she wearing? What did she look like? What was she doing?" Those are details that don't need to be shared. On the flip side, if there are things you are wondering about, feel free to ask.

There have been conversations regarding certain specifics that began with me saying, "You don't have to answer this if you don't want to..." I know some people may think me offering my husband an out in not having to answer questions is not the way to go. Some may say that he needs to answer any question I ask; he's the offender and I am the victim. I understand that way of thinking, to a point. But when it comes to some specifics, I stay away, and for good reason.

Johnnie has told me before that one reason he doesn't want to give me any details whenever he has slipped up is because it is so embarrassing just confessing that he messed up. He feels so ashamed of his actions, and he doesn't want to bring them up. I respect that. If it were me, I would want my spouse to give me a little dignity. You may think that your husband doesn't deserve this treatment, but you still must give them respect. I know many people say that respect is earned, but I beg to differ. We offer respect no matter who the person is, whether they deserve it or not.

In a marriage, respect is vital to the man. You can give your spouse the respect he craves without sacrificing accountability. Like I said, I don't ask for details of what Johnnie looked at or what he was picturing in his mind; however, I do hold him responsible for telling me other specifics like what device he used and the time of day it happened. He doesn't get a pass on those details. If we are going to be accountable there must be honesty and a willingness to be open. However, that doesn't mean you get to treat your spouse however you like.

When it comes to communication, expect your husband to discuss some basic information about the indiscretion, and don't be afraid to ask additional questions, but don't demoralize your spouse. Remember, you are a team. While you are still feeling hurt, you aren't going to retaliate. You are going to handle this with the nature that God gave you as a woman. Let me explain.

To find where a woman is first discussed in the Bible, it takes us all the way back to the beginning—the book of Genesis. God makes the statement in Genesis 2:18 NIV, "It is not good for the man to be alone. I will make a helper suitable for him." Now, as women who have husbands who are struggling with pornography, we KNOW this verse to be true! We know that when a man is alone, temptation comes. God warned us early on and created woman from that revelation! I say that slightly joking.

Some versions translate that verse to say that it is not beneficial for man to be alone. Thus, God created someone (woman) who is suitable, fit, or one who balances him out and is complementary to him. We, women, were created for such a beautiful purpose. We weren't created as second best, but we were created because after all the animals were created and after man was created, God realized that something was still missing. Planet earth and man wasn't complete without woman, so we were formed—formed for a specific purpose—to be a helper and companion. I find it interesting that when God said that it wasn't good for man to be alone, the word "good" is the same word that He used in the creation account after completing a day's work. Almost as if saying, man is incomplete without his helper.

The verse goes on to say that women were meant to be a help. When you hear that verse, do you ever imagine it as a parent to a child calling them your little helper? Unfortunately, that is the connotation that I read it as for a long time. I am JUST the helper. I wasn't the important one, just the helper. As a parent, there are things I can accomplish much quicker by myself, but my young kids want to help, so I let them be my little helpers. I don't need them to help, but they want to be there. And while I adore my kids, sometimes it is much easier doing these jobs by myself. Most parents know when their young children help it usually takes longer and they have to re-do a few things. It is that type of "help" that I always read into this verse.

I always knew I had skills and value as a woman, but reading this verse made me feel like I was "less than" in some way. The good news is that this is NOT the kind of help this verse is referring to. You are not just the little helper that is adored, but really not needed for the job. You are needed. In fact, the same word that is used in describing the woman as being the "helper" is the same word that is used throughout the Bible in referring to the help and deliverance that only God can bring. That changes the understanding of Genesis 2:18 completely! You are here under the divine purpose from God to be the helper, the companion who is fit for your husband. You aren't unnecessary or unwanted, but you are needed. It is you, your presence as a woman that turns the situation from something that God said was not good, into something that is good, necessary, beneficial, and complete.

You were created for a purpose and while you shouldn't

bear the burden of being responsible for your husband's free-dom, know that you are instrumental to his change. He must make the choice, but you can be divinely given human help to encourage and spur him on. It all starts with effective commu-nication.

B.C. (Before Communicating)

Where does effective communication start? With your-self. I know, it sounds counter-intuitive. But before you and your husband talk through this issue, there are a few things that need to happen within yourself first. The first thing to remem-ber is that you are not perfect and that you may have issues that need to be dealt with, too. It may not be as dramatic as a porn addiction, but you may still have things in your life that you know are not Godly, or areas where you are struggling. While these things have different consequences, they are still similar in that we are missing the mark that God has set for us to live by. I like how the Amplified Version translates Matthew 7:1-3

Do not judge and criticize and condemn [others unfairly with an attitude of self-righteous superiority as though assuming the office of a judge], so that you will not be judged [unfairly]. For just as you [hypocritically] judge others [when you are sinful and unrepentant], so will you be judged; and in accordance with your standard of measure[used to pass out judgment], judgment will be measured to you. Why do you look at the [insignificant] speck that is in your brother's eye, but do not notice and acknowledge the[egregious] log that is in your own eye?"

Please do not fall into the trap that says that your husband's sin is worse than your own. Is his bad? Yep. But is it forgivable? Also, yes. As is your own sin. A lesson learned the hard way (not recommended), look inward first before having an in-depth discussion with your spouse. And be willing to discuss your own imperfections with him as he is being honest with you. For instance, this conversation could play out something like this, "I know you're struggling with porn, and I know I'm not always perfect either. Whether we've talked about it much or not, I really struggle with _____. I never want to come across like I'm condemning you when I'm still working on myself, too."

It's important to avoid a sin hierarchy where you place yourself on a pedestal with your husband groveling at your feet. This may sound extreme, but I've learned some lessons the hard way and I've seen other women treat their husbands as sub-human and that is not a constructive way to face this issue. Sure, you may get results treating your husband like dirt, but it isn't going to be the long-term results you really want. Take some time and prayerfully consider the areas in which you are weak and commit to fighting in those areas the same way in which your husband is fighting.

In our marriage, eventually, we talked about one of the issues I have had to deal with, fear. While some people may not see that as a big deal, or even a sin, I beg to differ. Fear leads to worry and both fear and worry have their roots in not trusting God. Fear and not trusting God are exactly what the Israelites dealt with in the book of Numbers. It was their lack of faith and belief that kept them in the desert for 40 years before they crossed into the Promised Land. So yes, fear is a big deal, and you can't let it fester. My husband's knowledge of things I have been dealing with gave us joint accountability. When I ask him how he has been doing with porn temptation, he will ask me how I have been fighting fear. We will discuss this more in the next section, but I wanted to lay the foundation, now.

It is paramount that we, the wives, are in right standing with God, and that we are not being held captive by any stronghold. I say this not so you can rub it in your husband's face, but so we each can be right with God. Our lives are not a competition to see who is closer to God or who has less sin. Your life is meant to be lived walking in intimacy with God and living life in intimacy with your spouse. As you just read, you are here for a purpose. You are your husband's help. Not his inferior partner, but his God-given help. Before any discussion begins with your husband, you need to be right with God. It's not right to be accusing him of his wrongdoing when you aren't living right, either. Take some time and pray. Ask God to reveal the areas where you need to improve. I'm not suggesting that you must be perfect before you and your spouse talk, but I am suggesting that you need to be taking steps to fight any areas of imperfection in your life, just as you are asking and expecting your husband to do the same.

Your sin may not affect your husband as porn affects you. For instance, the fearful thoughts I had didn't impact Johnnie, it was a personal mental battle that I was fighting. Whereas his porn problem really impacted the way I felt, thought, and the way we acted toward each other. But just because my battle didn't affect him doesn't mean it was something to dismiss.

There isn't a lot of teaching on holiness right now. There is a lot of preaching of God's grace and His love, both of which are vitally important. But there comes a time when believers shouldn't be held captive to sin but should be pursuing holiness. I hope you are already there. I hope the process of introspection doesn't take you long because you are a committed follower of Christ who is always striving to be more like Christ and less like the world. If you aren't there yet and you do have things you need to work through, then do it! Remember, you are dead to sin, as Romans 6 says. You don't have to do what your fleshly desires want you to. You can live victoriously over every sin.

To summarize, recognize any areas where you are struggling, pray about them, and be willing to discuss those with your husband. You don't want your husband to feel alienated, you want him to feel willing to talk with you and be open with you. Secret sin loves alienation because there is no one there to shed light on it. However, when we decide to stop alienating ourselves and be vulnerable and let someone in, hidden sin can't hide anymore. Craig Groeschel said in one of his sermons, "Where secrecy lives, intimacy dies." As I have said many times already, your husband's addiction to porn is not okay. It is sin and it needs to be made right for the sake of himself, his relationship with God, his relationship with you, and his relationship with the rest of the family. However, we are quite instrumental in helping our husbands overcome this struggle. In your hurt, you must still love. In your pain, you must still encourage. In your despair, you must still pray for him.

Prayer is another thing to discuss regarding communication. You may not be able to control when you and your spouse discuss his porn addiction, that is why you must be prayerful about the conversation, whenever it may happen. I'm sure you have conversations in your head, much like I do. I'm sure there are times you have imagined how a conversation would go and you figured out exactly what you would say and what he would say and how you would respond, and on and on. While it is good to prepare, don't let your conscious thought regarding the conversation replace prayer.

In an unrelated matter, I was worried about a serious conversation I had to have with a close family member. I kept rehearsing how the conversation might go in my head over and over. I was going over the different responses that could happen and how I would respond. Finally, I felt God was telling me, "If you prayed about this conversation even half the time that you have spent worrying about it then..." and He didn't have to finish. The point was made. Instead of taking the matter to God, I was staying in my head trying to figure it out in my own power. So, I implore you, take it to God in prayer. Let God know your frustrations and worries about talking with your husband. Ask Him for help in remaining calm and clear-minded. Ask Him for guidance for the right words to be spoken. Ask Him for His peace in the situation. In Philippians 4:5-7 AMP the Bible says:

"Let your gentle spirit [your graciousness, unselfishness, mercy, tolerance, and patience] be known to all people. The Lord is near. Do not be anxious or worried about anything, but in everything [every circumstance and situation] by prayer and petition with thanksgiving, continue to make your [specific] requests known to God. And the peace of God [that peace which reassures the heart, that peace] which transcends all understanding, [that peace which] stands guard over your hearts and your minds in Christ Jesus [is yours].

What can we glean from these verses? First, notice the part of the gentle spirit. If you read the term "gentle spirit" but didn't know what it meant, you may keep reading thinking it may have no bearing on this topic. But as the amplified version explains, it refers to our graciousness, unselfishness, mercy, tolerance, and patience. Those qualities certainly apply to the given circumstance. In fact, those qualities are usually the antithesis of the emotions we are feeling! However, we are still to exhibit these qualities in our conversations. Next, it says not to be anxious or worried, once again, those feelings aren't natural during our time of turmoil. But we are to make our request known to God by prayers, petitions, and thanksgiving.

What's the difference between prayers and petitions? I've read many different opinions as to what this terminology means seeing as how it is easy to think the terms prayer and petition are interchangeable. These terms are not the same, but they are related. Many say that prayer is a general term for general prayer, and petitions or supplications is a more specific time of targeted requests. As you are praying and petitioning God, remain thankful. Obviously, it's not that you are thankful that your husband has been mentally undressing women with his eyes, but thankful that God is still there and still at work in the situation. Thank Him in advance for what He is going to do in the situation.

I understand that you don't know exactly how the situation is going to turn out. You don't know if your husband is going to be instantaneously delivered, never to have a lustful thought again, or maybe he will gradually get better, but the mental battle is one he must fight day to day. Or perhaps he won't change, what if he decides he wants to live for himself and continue to indulge in this self-destructive behavior? One thing will remain constant—God will never leave you or forsake you (Hebrews 13:5). Even on the darkest of days, even if things don't change, you will always have God and that is something to be thankful for.

You can also be thankful that God is going to give you the words to say and that He will give peace to you both in this situation. Just because a situation isn't peaceful doesn't mean that you can't have peace of mind in the midst of the circumstances. The many times Johnnie has confessed his indiscretions to me, I've had a variety of internal (and external) reactions. However, the more I have prayed about this situation, sought God, and sought to understand Johnnie, the more peace I have had about it. Instead of feeling like this was something that was never going to change, it changed in that I was starting to see small improvements. When he would have small victories, we would celebrate those. I had this inner confidence that this issue was going to change. It wasn't going to remain the same and it wasn't going to get worse, but with God's help, he was going to overcome this.

I don't want to assure you that your husband will change, because that is an assurance I can't make, and neither can you. The only person that can make the decision to do something about the issue is your husband. At some point, he must decide to take steps to change. Do I believe in supernatural deliverance? 100%. Can God do anything? Of course! But your husband still must make the choice not to be drawn in again.

Notes:

1. Hitch. DVD. New York, NY: Columbia, 2005.

10.
Communication: Part 2

F or us, the porn discussion didn't happen just once. This has been a long ordeal for Johnnie to go through, so we have had many discussions. And while I don't like that this has dragged on, having multiple conversations has been helpful. First, there were many times I had to go back and reevaluate myself, spend time in prayer, and make sure I was staying close to God before I jumped into any conversations about Johnnie's addiction or slip-ups. I would also spend time thinking and praying about what needed to be discussed and how I should approach the matter. Secondly, it's not a fun conversation for either party to have. Just about every time the topic would come up, one or both of us would say, "I hate talking about this." And it's not that we didn't want this to come to an end, but rather a dissatisfaction that this conversation had to happen because of his sin.

If you haven't spent much time talking to your spouse about his addiction to porn, let me first say, be prepared to be emotional. We have had conversations in which I thought I was going to be able to get through without tears or erupting in anger and frustration. But, twenty minutes and a box of tissues later, I realized I was wrong in my assumption. Emotions can rise within you quickly, so be aware that it will probably happen—and that's okay. Despite the emotions that you or your husband may be experiencing, the spirit in which you need to have any discussions about the matter is one of understanding, grace, and mercy. Once again, not because this behavior is okay, but because outbursts of anger aren't going to be fruitful. Rather, those types of outbursts will lead to more walls being put up and more hurtful speech being spewed.

Another lesson I learned the hard way: The times I reacted in anger and harshness are the times Johnnie had the hardest times recovering from his relapses. Recently, I asked him to articulate the importance of me or any wife reacting with understanding and grace, and this is what he had to say:

JOHNNIE: "When you confess to your spouse that you are looking at porn, you are already beating yourself up. You are making yourself vulnerable by confessing—taking down all your protection and being honest. Your spouse can take any shot they want, and it can really hurt you."

I never realized the power I held in how I reacted. You, too, hold the power, not so you can flaunt it over your husband, but be aware that how you react will have a bearing on how he responds. As the two of you discuss these matters, probably over multiple conversations, remember to be understanding and full of grace and mercy.

Are you hurting? Of course, but just because you are

hurt doesn't mean that you get to hurt your spouse in retaliation. I don't think I'm the only one who has ever noticed that in conversations, people tend to match the other person's tone and body language. So, if you are able to stay levelheaded and calm, chances are that your husband will also remain calm. However, if you erupt in anger expect him to match that same emotion during the discussion.

Your Feelings

Please know that your pain, frustration, hopelessness, anger—it all matters. I know I have mentioned a couple of times the need to put your emotions on the "back burner" of sorts. But you matter. And now, finally comes the time for us to talk about how to discuss your feelings with your husband. Your spouse probably knows that his actions hurt you, but there comes a time when you need to communicate those feelings to him to ensure he understands what you have been dealing with. To best do that, you need to understand them yourself. Luckily, early on Johnnie never asked me why his looking at porn hurt me. If he did, I might have responded by saying, "Uh, because it just does, okay!" Then go cry my eyes out. I began to ask myself, "Why does this bother me? Was it the betrayal of trust? The feeling of inadequacy I had now? Was it the fact that he had been looking at other women? Was it the lying?" And the answer—yes! It was all of it. As I am sure it is for you too.

Just as we didn't have one conversation about his addiction, so it was about my emotions and how I was feeling. Rather, it was smaller ones over the course of months. Over that time, I was able to articulate my feelings. A lot of the feelings I was having were based on the statements we explored in a previous chapter. Statements that were really based on lies or misinformation. Hopefully, you will have the time to evaluate how you feel and why you feel the way you feel before any discussions happen.

At times, it was challenging for me to discuss my feelings with Johnnie. It wasn't because I didn't want to be open and vulnerable with him, it was more out of caution for how he was going to take it. There were times I so desperately wanted to tell him how badly this addiction was hurting me, but I also realized something else—this addiction was hurting him, too.

Ultimately, I told him how I felt, but I was also very careful in those discussions because I didn't want to pile my emotional hurt onto him and then have him feel he has this unspoken responsibility to fix it. I know my husband, like most men, wants to fix the issue. I don't want him to try to "make it up" to me to fix it, and I definitely didn't want him to stop telling me what was going on, so my feelings weren't hurt. I simply wanted him to get rid of those the thoughts, the actions, and the addiction, permanently. That was the only fix.

So, how do you do that? How do you communicate about your feelings effectively? Well, to answer that I reference again the chapters about understanding the lies and misinformation. Understanding the root cause can be helpful.

I found that having short, focused conversations about my feelings usually worked better for us. So, when I mentioned I would be careful in the discussions we had, what I mean is that I tried not to overwhelm Johnnie with everything I was feeling at that moment. I might just focus on one aspect of what I was facing. For us, that worked well. I would rather explain my emotions over the course of smaller conversations so Johnnie could process that particular conversation and not try to remember the list of feelings I poured out to him. For instance, I may tell him that I was feeling very discouraged and then explain why I felt discouraged. Now, was I also feeling sad, hurt, betrayed, etc.? Yes. And we talked about all those things over the course of different conversations. But I would rather focus on something small and make sure I do a good job communicating that particular aspect rather than go on a rant and neither of us remembers anything I said.

I've referenced this previously, but I want to mention it again, taking those overcoming feelings to the Lord is the only effective way to experience healing. If you have placed your hope and your spouse in the Lord's hands and you are experiencing His peace about the situation, you will be able to talk to your husband (somewhat) calmly about how you feel, and you will have the confidence that only the Lord can give.

His Feelings

With all the feelings and emotions and doubts swirling around in our heads, no wonder it can be complicated to communicate effectively. There are times when you and your spouse are not on the same page, you may not even be in the same book! That's why it is important to pick your battles. Within a conversation, you may have many thoughts going through your head giving a rebuttal to what your husband is saying, but sometimes you need to take a step back and think before you speak. When there is an argument, it's easy to become defensive whether we are correct or not. We automatically jump into competition mode where we are trying to "win". That mindset can lead to some regretful rhetoric coming from our mouths. Our marriages are not a competition. It isn't a challenge to see who is right more often or who is putting in more effort. As my former pastor said, marriage isn't 50-50, it's 100-100—each person giving 100%.

Unfortunately, society has played a good hand in convincing everyone that the wife is always right. It's so common to hear, and now many people joke about it. I'm not sure about your household, but in this house, the wife is not always right. And sometimes I need to keep my mouth shut and let my husband tell me how he's feeling without me trying to explain why he is wrong or to try to top his story. Anyone else? I know I'm not the only one guilty of doing that.

We want our husbands to listen to us and engage in conversation with us about our feelings, but sometimes we don't offer them the same courtesy. As related to porn, this tends to happen because we feel like we are the victim. In reality, you are both hurting, just in different ways. So, whether you are in a confrontation about porn, or just in general conversation, give your spouse time to talk and express his feelings, even if it's not a topic you find interesting.

We've all been in conversations when the other person tries to delegitimize our feelings. I know I have been guilty of doing the same to Johnnie. I have had to remind myself that I don't have to have an explanation for everything he says, sometimes I just need to listen. Meaning, when he says he's tired, I don't need to respond with, "Oh, you're tired? I was up with the baby until 2 AM, then up with our oldest at 5 AM, then slept for another 2 hours before the middle one was ready to get up." There is definitely a time to express those things, so both sides understand what the other is going through, but sometimes in the heat of the moment isn't the best time.

For instance, shortly after we had our third child, we

took a trip to our favorite state park to swim and enjoy some family time after dinner. Johnnie had our two boys wading in the water, and I was sitting on the shore with our newborn baby girl. The boys had a blast in the water. But our time there quickly deteriorated, as the closer it got to bedtime the worse our children were behaving. By the time we got home and got the kids in bed, Johnnie and I were in a little spat. He told me that he was frustrated because he felt there were many times he must fight for my attention because I am too focused on the kids. The conversation went on and he was explaining his side of the story.

Meanwhile, I was fuming on the inside, ready to fire back with multiple reasons as to why his feelings were wrong. There were interactions that led to our spat that we were trying to talk out at the same time, and while Johnnie was explaining how he felt in monologue fashion, I was picking his reasoning apart and already arguing with him in my head. I had some good points to throw back in his face, as soon as I got the chance to explain my side.

Thankfully, none of the comments I was thinking made it out of my head. It would have been so easy to let one of those comments fly, which would have led to more of an argument, instead of getting to a solution. However, it was important that I gave him time to talk and express what he was feeling. Instead of telling him that he was misguided in his assumptions—which wasn't necessarily the case anyway—or trying to story top by explaining the competition I have for his attention, I just listened. I asked questions when appropriate and apologized for doing things that made him feel that way.

Now, is it important that he understands the challenges of raising and caring for small children? Of course! Should you neglect your feelings just to avoid conflict and end an argument? No! When we were both calmer and the situation de-escalated, I explained more of the feelings I had in a much calmer way than I would have if I would have said those things in the moment. Not only was I able to accurately communicate my feelings, but he was also in a better place to listen to what I had to say because I had already listened and tried to understand his feelings. We ended that evening both committed to approaching things in a way in which neither of us would feel we would have to fight for the attention of the other, while recognizing that we both have other responsibilities.

Even after years of marriage, we are still learning to communicate and to communicate in a considerate way, whether it's about porn or just about daily life. It's quite easy to assume your spouse means something, when in fact the opposite is true. When you aren't communicating effectively, this difference in understanding can cause confusion and pain. Now, I'm not suggesting that you speak to each other on a first-grade level, but I am suggesting that you explain your feelings clearly and make sure your spouse knows what you mean by any subjective terms that are used. Lastly, as a general tip, if possible, don't have important conversations when you are overly tired or know you are emotionally volatile. We all have those days when we know that we could "blow" at any moment, and that is not the time to have an important discussion regarding your marriage.

So, what do you do if you find yourself on the cusp of a conversation, but you are feeling like you may say something you will regret? Be honest. Honesty has been such a refreshing reality in our marriage. Not just related to the struggle of porn, but in general conversation Johnnie and I have been honest enough to admit when we aren't listening and ask the other to repeat what was just said. It would be much easier to nod and say, "uh-huh". But instead, we have chosen to be honest and if we aren't listening, we tell the other person so we can stay engaged in the conversation.

Luckily, this has allowed for honesty in important conversations as well. There have been many times when instead of arguing, we have agreed that if we started to talk about that topic now, we'd just end up fighting. Rather than jump into a fight, we talk at a different time. At least, that is the preferred Method. It is pointless to go into an important discussion when you know it won't end well based on the moods of those involved.

When we first were married, we had to learn how to fight and how to handle volatile conversations. It took quite a few arguments for us to learn our different styles of fighting. Arguments would come and Johnnie, determined to fight his way, would want to get it all out in the open then and there. So much so that one time during our first year of marriage, he followed me through the house trying to continue the argument. All the while, I was trying to fight my way. My way is vastly different than Johnnie's. I don't want to say everything I'm feeling at the moment because I know I'll say something I regret and usually something I don't mean just so I can win the argument! Typically, I want to get away for a few minutes and pray so I won't be a jerk and say something untrue. I don't remember what the argument was about that day, but we both remember the time he was chasing me through the house trying to argue and I was running away trying to be by myself so I could think and pray. That argument was a turning point, and since then we both understand how the other handles an argument. It has made it easier because he knows I need a few minutes, and I know that he wants to make sure we communicate about what is bothering us as soon as possible and not let it fester.

I don't mention all these things in anticipation of you and your spouse fighting, but I do know how quickly these conversations can escalate. Why is that? Well, you both are experiencing a lot of frustration, you are feeling hurt, he's feeling like it's all his fault and he can't stop, you may be feeling responsible in some way and neither of you wants to feel wronged in the situation! So, I mention these stories for two reasons. The first reason is so hopefully you will avoid an unnecessary argument by choosing an appropriate time to discuss his problem with porn.

Secondly, to mention the importance of prayer in an argument or even just a volatile conversation. You may not have heard anyone say that they pray before or during an argument, but I do. I have done this almost all our married life and it has been the most helpful way to end an argument. So, just in case you don't know what that looks like, here's what it looks like for me. If we are still in the same room together, I silently pray something like, "God, how can we make this right and stop this argument? What do I need to do? Am I in the wrong?" I usually then explain my frustration to God and wait and see how He responds. There are times when I have immediate clarity and know I was wrong and need to apologize to Johnnie. There are other times when I wasn't necessarily in the wrong, but I didn't handle the conversation in the best way and still, I need to make it right. Other times, I may not necessarily need to apologize, but I need to approach the situation differently. I need to approach the circumstance with grace and understanding instead of harshness.

Unfortunately, arguments happen. Occasionally, they

can be the result of good communication because you are talking about what you want or need. However, more often they are the result of poor communication because assumptions are made that may not be correct.

Dealing with pornography has been a much longer road than either of us wanted or expected. We haven't had one conversation about the basic details and then never had to discuss the matter again. Because Johnnie kept getting pulled back in, he kept looking at porn over and over and we had many discussions about the circumstances around his indiscretions.

The Specifics

While the specifics of each conversation were different, eventually we would discuss certain standard details. The first thing he would tell me is when it happened. As he grew further away from being considered an addict and it became more of an occasional struggle, I began to get curious to see if there was a pattern. For instance, was I home or had I gone out for a quick errand? Was I away on a trip? What time of day did it happen? Of course, a pattern emerged. It would usually happen when I was gone. Simple solution, right? I'll just never leave! Of course, that's not realistic nor is it how you want your spouse to be rid of his addiction.

As Johnnie has gotten closer and closer to being rid of this giant, his slip-ups were more sporadic, and it was only if I was gone multiple days. And yes, we had filters in place and websites blocked, but unfortunately, once an image has been viewed, it stays in the mind. And that is what has made this struggle so hard to put to bed. He may not be actively searching out pornography, but something will trigger him, and those images are already in his head. Just like you can with some electronics, it makes me wish I could rub a strong magnet on his head so it would erase the images! But I don't think that would be effective.

That leads me to the next thing that is discussed: Which device was used. Phone? TV? Computer? Tablet? Technology is wonderful, until it comes to the porn struggle, then it is incredibly frustrating. While filters do help, as I just mentioned with Johnnie, sometimes it doesn't matter if a filter is there if the images are already in his head. Nonetheless, ask him what he used. If a pattern emerges, then you can look at ways to have stronger filters or other practical means to help avoid a relapse.

It may sound odd to ask what time of day, but temptation tends to be strongest when we are tired, hungry, or frustrated. At those points we are weak and may not have the resolve needed to fight. I mentioned this earlier in the book, but it is worth repeating. If your husband continually has a hard time right when he gets home from work, then you may need to encourage him to re-evaluate his routine.

AD (After the Dialogue)

I hate having the porn talk with my husband. I know it makes him uncomfortable and it makes me uncomfortable, too. In some ways, it gets easier talking about it the more times you have to talk about it. However, I don't want this to be a long-drawn-out issue for you, so I hope you don't get too comfortable talking about it. During the conversations, it shouldn't be a scripted conversation where you are interrogating him. It should be a dialogue. One where you talk about what happened, how he is feeling, explain how you're feeling, and try to figure out where to go next. During these conversations, I would usually ask him if there was anything I could do to help. Sometimes he would tell me there was nothing I could do. Other times, he would tell me that I need to ask him more often how he has been doing with the issue.

Most importantly, don't continue to hold this against your husband. Growing up, I didn't understand what condemnation was. I had heard verses from the Bible about it but didn't know what it was. What I did know is that when I sinned, I felt bad. And I felt that God stayed mad at me until I "worked off" my bad deeds. I still remember driving home one day frustrated about something I had done, when it hit me—I've confessed it and God doesn't hold it against me. I don't have to keep re-hashing it in my mind. Nor do I have to "work off" my sin before God will love me again. God loves me. PERIOD. Since God loves me and has chosen to forgive me, I will continue to forgive my husband over and over again. I know we have talked about that already, but just in case your husband has had a relapse since that chapter and you've been tempted to stay mad, here's your reminder: Don't do it!

When Johnnie confesses and apologizes, I let it go immediately. We talk about whatever needs discussing (when, where etc.) and evaluate if we need to tighten up his permissions on his devices, then we move on to a different topic. I don't make him work off his bad deeds to get in my good graces again, just as God doesn't do that with us. Johnnie and I are immediately reconciled. To be honest, I try to get us talking about something fun soon after so we can move on and not dwell on it. Dwelling on the matter will not help.

I know that every situation is different. You may be frustrated right now because perhaps your husband is indifferent to your feelings and seems like he doesn't care to stop. We'll be addressing this later in this book. For now, don't stop trying to communicate with him. It's easy to get discouraged and give up. But keep going. Keeping setting a good example of what healthy communication looks like.

To finish this section, let's revisit what communication is. We said it is the process of sending, receiving, and understanding a message. When you are talking about an issue as important as this, please make sure you are communicating clearly. Make sure you are understanding what each other actually means, not just what you think they mean. As women, sometimes we tend to send hints and hope our husbands get them. We hope they will pick up on our subtleties, but let's face it, it doesn't always happen. Don't rely on subtleties, be clear. If you're sad, be honest and tell him you are sad. Be willing to be open with each other, forgiving, and committed to seeing this addiction end. Clear communication is key, and it is vital when your spouse is struggling.

11.

Is Pornography Idolatry?

ould you believe me if I said that pornography, prostitution, and idolatry were linked? It's not a connection that you would naturally make, but when looking at the Biblical accounts, their association is undeniable. To see this begin to unfold, we're going to take a step back into history. In the 8th century BC, Rome was just being founded and Homer had written his epics, the *Iliad* and the *Odyssey*. It is during this time period we read of the prophecies of Hosea. And if anyone in the Bible can identify with having a spouse with unfaithful sexual tendencies, Hosea is the man. Hosea's book is a small book, called a minor prophet, sandwiched between Daniel and Joel in the Old Testament. He prophesied to the northern kingdom of Israel from approximately 750 BC to 715 BC. He was on the scene before and during the deportation of the northern kingdom of Israel to Assyria in 722 BC.

In case you have no idea what I'm talking about, here's

a quick Bible history lesson. Early in the Bible, you have the story of Moses and the Israelites. They leave Egypt to go to the land flowing with "milk and honey," which is what we know as Israel. Moses eventually died and passed the torch to Joshua who led the Israelites into this land and conquered the people groups in this area, just as God had promised. Fast forward to the time of David, as in David and Goliath, who was King over Israel for 40 years, around 1000 BC. At this point in history, Israel was one united kingdom. While they weren't perfect, this era is said to be the pinnacle of Israel's history. After David's son Solomon reigned and died, the nation split into two kingdoms, the northern kingdom of Israel and the southern kingdom of Judah. From there, things went downhill. Immoral king after king rose to power in each kingdom and led the people away from God. Idolatry was rampant during this period. The two kingdoms—Israel and Judah were eventually conquered by outside enemies, just as the prophets said they would, because the Israelites did not stay faithful to the Lord. These two kingdoms were conquered at different times. Our man, Hosea, prophesied to the northern kingdom of Israel, as mentioned, before they were captured and taken into foreign captivity at the hands of the Assyrians.

Why is it that we can identify with Hosea? Well, God gave him a special mandate to marry a woman who was going to be unfaithful to him. There is some debate as to whether she was a prostitute when he married her or whether she turned to prostitution after they were wed. Either way, she was unfaithful to Hosea while he remained loving and ever-faithful.

God told Hosea to marry Gomer as an example to the nation of Israel of the love that God has for his people. God's message? Even though Israel had forsaken the covenant with

God, He still loved her and was committed to her. We learn from the book of Hosea that as the nation of Israel grew, so did their idolatry. They would seek other gods, such as Ba'als and Asherahs instead of the one true God. They would still do some of the religious routines associated with serving God, but in their hearts, they were far from Him. They weren't spiritually pure. They had a mixture of worshiping God and worshiping the foreign Canaanite gods.

Right now, it may be tough to see how porn relates to idolatry, as I assume you probably view idolatry much like I did. My first legitimate exposure to idol worship, as I commonly think of it, was during a religio-cultural field trip I took in college. I attended a Christian college and for this trip, we traveled to an area in Ohio that had a variety of different practicing religions. We visited many different places of worship, and one such place was a Hindu temple. We entered the area where their gods were placed and the gentleman showing us around the temple began to explain the different rituals to us. I don't remember exactly how many gods were in this particular room, but there were quite a few. Each of the idol statues were ornately dressed. On the floor near the idols, I noticed a pie tin filled with milk, with an apple placed inside. The guide informed us that they placed the milk and the apple there as food for their deities. I asked what happened when their food offering wasn't consumed. He replied that the gods just weren't hungry. I was somewhat surprised by his answer. It seemed obvious to me that if you constantly leave food for your god and he/she doesn't eat it, then perhaps he doesn't exist. The guide justified their lack of appetite by explaining that the gods consumed the sacrifice at another temple. Having this exposure not only to this temple, but the many different places of worship we visited, gave me a practical example of idol worship.

While idolatry may have the connotation of an obvious affront to the worship of God, such as the temple I visited, that may not always be the case. You don't have to be wearing an "I love Buddha" shirt around to be guilty of idolatry. Depending on which translation of the Bible you read, you may see a different term used when discussing idolatry. One such term is graven image. A "graven image" is the same thing as an idol, it is just a different word. Thus, I always focused idolatry on the image itself, like the images or statues I saw in Ohio.

Without realizing it, my thinking was that you can only be guilty of idolatry if there is a statue to which you are bowing. Rather, it isn't completely about the image in and of itself, but the imagination behind it. It's about what you are submitting or attaching yourself to, and what you are committing to serve. If you are submitting and serving only yourself despite God's commands, then you would be guilty of making yourself an idol. I've done some research on idolatry while writing this book, and one thing I consistently found was the Old Testament focused on worshiping images other than God. However, the New Testament doesn't focus quite as much on the image itself, but rather the imagination.[1] Interestingly enough, image and imagination are remarkably similar words. Another author puts it as, "The Old Testament focuses on actual idol worship, while the New Testament takes aim at the desires that underlie idolatry." [2] In Ezekiel 14:3 NLT, the Bible says, "Son of man, these leaders have set up idols in their hearts. They have embraced things that will make them fall into sin. Why should I listen to their requests?" Here we see the Bible mention that you can have an idol that is in your heart, and not one that you are physically bowing to. So, if you can make idols in your heart, you can easily see how the outward bowing to idols is just a physical expression of an inward commitment you've already made to something other than the God of the Bible.

Two things led to this section. The first came while reading through the book of Hosea as I was going through my Bible reading. I got to Hosea 4 and felt the Holy Spirit quicken my spirit. I knew the book and specifically, that chapter had something to do with the porn struggle. Around that same time, I was asking Johnnie questions and he compared the porn struggle to one having an idol.

Unfortunately, there isn't a big focus on idolatry in the church today. Because it is rarely taught about, many are guilty of the same assumption that I was, if it isn't a wooden or stone object to which you are bowing, then it's not really idolatry. But was Johnnie's comparison true? Can pornography be an idol? Can money be an idol? Can pleasing people and a whole host of other desires be equated with bowing to the gods as the Israelites did in Hosea's time? To answer this question, I sought to have a deeper understanding of what idol worship really means.

If idolatry isn't simply bowing before a wooden idol or being a part of a different religion, then what is it? If the Israelites, God's own chosen people can be guilty, can we Christians be guilty as well? How does this all relate together? Can we be idolatrous and never have identified it as such? The answer is yes, we can be guilty of idolatry even if we are at church on Sunday. So, what is it exactly?

Edward Welch explains it like this, "Idolatrous desires typically start from a seed of desire that is natural and appropriate when kept in check. These desires could be for adequate finances, health, obedient children, inclusion, pleasure, rest, and justice. The key insight from Scripture is that these normal and even good desires tend to grow (James 1:15). As they gather strength, they battle against us like an unbound giant that finds little satisfaction (Eph. 4:19; James 4:1). Anytime our desires are aimed away from God, our hearts will be left wanting more." [3]

To paraphrase David Powlison's response to the question "What is idolatry", he says the word idolatry is simply a way of asking what am I doing with God or with something that isn't God when something bad is coming out of my life. He goes on to give an example of how someone may react when something bad happens—whether major or minor and brings it back to our desire to see our own will be done. He references Psalm 46:1 that says God is our refuge and strength and our help in affliction. "However, whenever I am in trouble in affliction I flip on the TV, or I go eat instead of turning to God. Behind my action, there is a spiritual action that is saying the ice cream or the TV or "my will be done" is driving it… I'm either worshiping and trusting the true God or something else. My actions… will show if I have tied myself to something else in my fallen nature." [4]

It is easy, then, to see pornography as a form of idolatry. As those lustful thoughts begin to demand satisfaction, those ensnared in porn's grips succumb to the images. Instead of trusting in God as their refuge and help and the one who satisfies them, or instead of allowing their wives to meet their needs, they turn to themselves as the answer and, in this case, the internet. Never thought about it that way? Me neither.

You may be thinking, what's the big deal though? Why does God care if we worship Him or not? Why does He require us to be faithful? I could turn the same question around to you, why is it a big deal if your husband is faithful? It's an easy answer, you love your spouse and desire that he is wholly committed to you, not splitting his affections with someone else.

God describes his relationship with Israel and eventually with the church as a marriage. We, the church, are the bride, and He is the husbandman. Marriage is the most intimate, special relationship you can have, as it was made to join two people forever. When we focus our attention toward other things than God, He gets jealous. He's not jealous in the sense of two kids fighting over toys. Rather, he is jealous because our worship rightly belongs to him.[5] When the Lord equates idolatry with prostitution it makes perfect sense. Prostitutes are giving what rightly belongs to their spouse, to someone else. I am my husband's, and he is mine. I give him myself, just as he does with me. Our sexuality isn't meant to be shared with anyone else.

The book of Hosea mainly focuses on the symbolism of the nation of Israel, but it is through the lens of the story of Hosea and Gomer. We know they had at least 3 children together, with some pretty interesting names. In fact, they were names that God gave them to be symbols of the coming judgment on the nation of Israel, such names meaning "not shown mercy" and "not my people". After that, we are told that Gomer left her married life with Hosea to pursue the lusts around her. She became a prostitute and eventually a slave.

Let's stop the story here for a moment. As a happily married woman with children, I wonder how any woman could consider doing that. But a similar scene is still being played out over 2,000 years later. Married couples call it quits after years of commitment and years of experiences binding them together. I wish it were rare, but it isn't. For some of these couples, there is seemingly nothing wrong and it is unexpected to their friends and family. Others know their spouse is struggling or perhaps there was already an affair, and they are trying to work it out, but there is another affair, and they call it quits. And this is where we can begin to see our story correlate with Hosea's.

You're married, then a choice is made, and compromise happens. Instead of being faithful, your spouse viewed porn. Maybe he tells you, maybe he doesn't. But then, it happens again and again and again. Perhaps this was an addiction he has had for years that you didn't know about, or maybe it is just forming. You are reading this so I can assume your spouse is probably tangled in an addiction that is causing everyone in your family pain. Yet, he still makes the choice to view the images and succumb to that temptation. Choosing to serve himself and give to something else that which belongs to you. He makes the choice to dwell on the thoughts and scenes he has seen instead of choosing to stay true to his wife and faithful to God. Sound familiar? Me too.

Let's remember, our husbands aren't just hurting us, but they are hurting God, too. Just as Gomer first left to pursue other lovers and eventually became a slave, so our spouses have left to pursue passion and have become a slave to those passions. John 8:34 AMP says, "Jesus answered, "I assure you and most solemnly say to you, everyone who practices sin habitually is a slave of sin.""

Unlike Gomer, for most of you, your spouse is probably still in your house. So, when I say spouses have left, I don't mean that they physically left, but there is a certain separation that happens when your spouse engages in porn. Emotionally, things aren't the same in light of a porn addiction. Physically, you may be living in the same house, but emotionally, there's a separation.

We have no idea what Gomer's motivation was for leaving Hosea. We have no idea how she was treated or if she was enjoying her new life away from her husband and children. If I had any guess, she probably wasn't too happy, seeing as she was a slave. And let's be honest, when we know we have made a big mistake, it can be hard to come back to the person you wronged. How many times have we heard some version of the story, "I want to go back, but I can't. She/he will never take me back..." We don't know if that was the case with Gomer and it may or may not be the case with your husband, but I can tell you that it is probably hard on your spouse knowing that he has this addiction. It may please him in the moment, but regret is probably following him as well. I know Johnnie has explained to me how heavy the guilt is afterward. The same voice that was prodding him to do it, was right back in his ear telling him how awful he was because he did it. And because of the guilt, he didn't want to talk about it or admit to it. He knew he had made the wrong decision, even though at the time it felt right.

Now, back to the story of Gomer and Hosea. Even then, God didn't forget Gomer or Hosea. Instead, God sent Hosea to purchase Gomer back from those enslaving her. Hosea redeemed her for a price, and they continued their marriage. There is a time in chapter 3 when Hosea brings her back home and tells her that she is going to be staying there, but she is to have no relations with any other man. He went on to say that eventually, the time of cleansing and punishment would end. In the Amplified Bible, it says in verse 3 that it would be this way "until [she] proved her faithfulness." Overall, it is an intense story. It's a storyline that you may expect to see in a movie, not in the Bible!

We are Hosea in this story. Hopefully, we are the ones

who are giving our spouse love, respect, and attention. We have been faithful (hopefully), while our spouse hasn't. At this point, we are in chapter 3 of their story. Your spouse may not have physically left the house, but he is bound. He is enslaved to his sin, as he is trapped in an addiction, just as Hosea's wife was enslaved. It amazes me that Gomer wasn't worried about hurting the feelings of her husband or abandoning her children. From the information given, she just left. You could say that she was blind to the consequences. And don't we see the same thing? I know I have asked Johnnie multiple times, "Didn't you think this was going to hurt me?" And he said it was in his mind, but it seemed to be so minor or downplayed, as if he was blind to my feelings, even though I would say he is the person who knows me best and cares for me the most. Johnnie's reaction is not the first one I have heard like that. I've heard many stories regarding different types of substance abuse where the user says they know it's bad and hurtful, but there is an element of blindness to the circumstance as they are not willing to change.

Finally, we see that Gomer had many lovers. She kept compromising and kept this sin going for an undisclosed amount of time. Johnnie has said that pornography keeps you going in circles. You are tempted and you give in, you have the immediate pleasure, but then regret soon follows. Then you feel down because you messed up and you feel the need to self-medicate. You know looking at porn again will fill that need, and bring you pleasure and relief from your frustration. This leads to another compromise.

I was reading a book that was referencing habitual sin and its effects on your family. The author mentions the story of Samson from the book of Judges in the Bible. At the end of his life, after Samson had compromised on all his commitments to

God, he is captured by the Philistines. At one point, he is at a mill grinding grain. In this time and culture, this was done by pushing a millstone around in a circle over the grain to crush it. So, Samson pushed the millstone around during his captivity. The author states that Sampson was "blind, bound and going 'round and 'round."[6]

When I read this, I thought it was such an accurate picture of the pornography bondage. And we see this acted out in Hosea as well. The person is blind to the effects of their sin, they are bound in their addiction, and they keep repeating the same actions, going around and around.

And what did Hosea do? Two things, first, he stayed close to the Lord. He didn't get lost in depression, but he stayed close to the Lord. Secondly, he acted. He bought her back. He went and paid a mixture of silver and materials to buy her back from slavery. Can you imagine what the ride or walk home must have been like? Was she thankful? Was she embarrassed? Did she want to go? Who knows! We have no idea what life was like after Gomer returned home. But Hosea went to Gomer's captor, paid the price, and brought her home. He was willing to forgive her abandonment, her sexual sin, her ignorance, and restore her to the position of his wife. It wasn't to fulfill a law and it sure wasn't for reputation, but it was because of love and obedience to the Lord.

According to Jewish law in Deuteronomy 22, Hosea should've stoned her, but he didn't. Instead, he did as God commanded him, and took her back. Remember, this story is also to show God's love for his people. No matter what angle you view this, from God's perspective or Hosea's, he brought her back because of love.

What does that mean for the countless women who find

themselves in the same position as yourself? The same position that I found myself in for longer than I expected. The wives who have been wronged, hurt, and in some sense abandoned. What are you going to do? What do you need to do? Obviously, there isn't a monetary amount to pay that magically releases your spouse from their bondage, as it was with Gomer's physical captors. But there is a correlation between Hosea's actions and what we can do.

First, you need to love your spouse in a redeeming way. Now, before you jump to conclusions and think that sounds like a cliché mom blog, let's evaluate what that means. I had heard the phrase "redeeming love" from different hymns growing up, and I even read the novel *Redeeming Love* by Francine Rivers. But after Johnnie's mom expressed to me one day her appreciation that I loved Johnnie in a redeeming way, it got me thinking more about that phrase. The concept of redemption is one of purchasing power. Come on ladies, we all know how to redeem a coupon! In the Bible, it mentions the process of redemption in both the Old and New Testaments. Looking at the New Testament, it is in reference to Jesus and how he redeemed us from sin. (Gal. 3:13, 4:5). And while I have no power to redeem Johnnie from sin, I can love him and pay a price "to help recover from the power of another," as Strong's Concordance defines the Greek word for redeem. It's a love that says, I'm not going to give up on you and I will always fight for you, and I will always forgive you. I will do whatever it takes to help you! In I Peter 4:8 AMP it says, "Above all, have fervent and unfailing love for one another, because love covers a multitude of sins [it overlooks unkindness and unselfishly seeks the best for others]."

You must be willing to pay the price. What price is

that? The price of commitment. The price that says, "I'm going to love you no matter what and I'm going to forgive you no matter what." The price that puts your feelings second to try to understand your spouse first. Now, I'm not saying that your feelings aren't important —trust me—but there have been times that instead of spouting off how I feel, I've just let Johnnie talk, or I've decided to wait to tell him what I'm feeling. As I've said in a previous chapter, my feelings are important, but there are times when I need to make sure the timing is right to communicate those feelings. Porn is always wrong, that part is always true. But taking the time to understand the other factors at play can go a long way in building trust and confidence between the two of you.

There may also be a monetary cost involved. For instance, you and your spouse may decide that talking to a marriage or family counselor is the best course of action. We've had friends go that route and it is what made the difference for them. Obviously, there is a cost associated with that. Or perhaps you want to get a filter for your internet and mobile devices. There is usually a monthly or annual cost for those services. So yes, there is an emotional and sometimes a physical price to pay, but it is worth it. As it was with Hosea and Gomer, there may be a period where things aren't going well, but those times will end, and restoration can happen. Thus, we come to the end of chapter 3 in Hosea and the end of what we know of the story of Gomer and Hosea. However, the book continues, and chapter 4 offers some interesting insight that applies to what we are discussing.

Notes:

1.Morris, Robert. "The Principle of Purity". YouTube, uploaded by Gateway Church TV, 25March 2017. https://www.youtube.com/Watch?v=-XMkPiDwx_8

2.Welch, Edward. "Addictions and Idolatry." Ligonier Ministries, 1 Aug. 2016, www.ligonier.org/learn/articles/addictions-and-idolatry/.

3.Ibid.

4.Powlison, David. "What Is Idolatry?" Christian Counseling & Educational Foundation, 27 Aug. 2020, www.ccef.org/video/what-idolatry/.

5.GotQuestions.org. "Why Is God a Jealous God?" GotQuestions.org, 13 May 2009, www.gotquestions.org/jealous-God.html.

6. Stone, Perry F. Purging Your House, Pruning Your Family Tree. Charisma House, 2011.

12.
Lessons from a Prostitute

Before we delve into chapter 4 of Hosea, I want to address something. Have you ever wondered why the Israelites were so quick to forsake the Lord? He brought them out of Egypt by miraculous means, fed them and supplied all their needs in the desert for 40 years, and gave them amazing victories in conquering their land, but still, they turned to the idols of the land they were now inhabiting.

It's been said that the inhabitants of Canaan were some of the most prolific idol worshipers. They fooled the Israelites into believing they needed to serve other gods by saying that they needed personal gods and household gods in addition to the god they served as their national god, Yahweh.[1] Another source has blamed Israel's desire to be like other nations as a contributing factor of their repeat idolatry.[2] And of course, one way the worship of these religions took place was by having sex with a temple prostitute. One focus of the Canaanite religion was fruitfulness, the fruitfulness of crops and the fruitfulness of the womb. So, we have the Israelites, a nation newly freed from Egyptian slavery, who not only witnessed the worship of numerous gods in the land of Egypt, yet they also saw the miraculous power of their own God. Then despite the warning given, they began to intermingle and intermarry with the nations and people in the land of Canaan. They witnessed the mighty works of God, but they also saw what people around them were doing and decided they wanted a little of both. Thus, they would still offer sacrifices to God, yet they would also go worship the gods of the Canaanites. God had already promised to bless and multiply their descendants, and He had promised to bless the land. The promises of God were already there, but instead of trusting the things that God had spoken to them as a nation, they took the popular route which led them into idolatry.

Just as I've mentioned before, here is another negative idea that hasn't changed over time. Not just in our sexuality, but in Christianity in general. As Christians, we have promises that God has given us. But for some reason, it's like many think that isn't good enough and instead pursue their own attempts to have a version of those blessings. As it relates to sexuality, God designed marriage to be exclusively between a committed husband and wife. Neither spouse is to seek out anyone or anything else to fulfill their sexual desires, other than their spouse.

The Bible gives us the standard, statistics tell us how we are measuring up to those standards, and they are painting quite a different story. Instead of marriages operating within the blessings that are the result of staying true to God's promises, many marriages are experiencing difficulty related to sexual compromise. Dr. Meg Meeker says, "Rates of sexual activity outside of marriage have changed so dramatically over the last seventy years that it would almost be fair to say that normalcy has been turned on its head."[3]

It can be tough trying to keep a pure mind when throughout the day you are inundated with images and suggestions from different types of media that try to rip committed marriages apart. Now, is that their goal? No, but their means of achieving whatever their goals are (high viewing rates, increase in sales, etc.) are leaning heavily on the sexual nature of humanity and they are willing to sacrifice marriage commitments to achieve their goals. Many have been quite desensitized by culture today, as the amount of sex in our media is staggering. We have had to turn the TV off many times because an inappropriate commercial has come on while we were watching an innocuous show. From the attire of some female announcers, to suggestive commercials, to comments in shows, things have changed, and while businesses may be getting more attention to their products, the minds and hearts of men and their families are being negatively affected.

Going into Hosea 4, we hear no more about Gomer and Hosea, but Hosea pens the word of the Lord to Israel. Verse one sums up what the entire chapter will be detailing, "Hear the word of the Lord, you children of Israel, For the Lord has a [legal] case with the inhabitants of the land, because there is no faithfulness [no steadfast love, no dependability] or loyalty or kindness or knowledge of God [from personal experience with Him] in the land." AMP From there it details the sin of Israel from the priests to the common man and begins to discuss some consequences of Israel's unfaithfulness. As we proceed through chapter 4, we get to verses 10-14. God has already mentioned the depravity of the priests and is now starting to discuss the common man. I'm going to include passages from two different versions. One from the Amplified version and the second from The Message paraphrase:

Hosea 4:10-14 AMP: They will eat, but not have enough; They will play the prostitute, but not increase [their descendants], Because they have stopped giving heed to the Lord. Prostitution, wine, and new wine take away the mind and the [spiritual] understanding. My people consult their [lifeless] wooden idol, and their [diviner's] wand gives them oracles. For a spirit of prostitution has led them astray [morally and spiritually], And they have played the prostitute, withdrawing themselves from their God. They sacrifice on the tops of the mountains and burn incense on the hills, under oaks, poplars, and terebinths, because the shade is pleasant there. Therefore, your daughters play the prostitute and your brides commit adultery. I will not punish your daughters when they play the prostitute or your brides when they commit adultery, for the men themselves slip away with prostitutes, and they offer sacrifices with temple prostitutes [who give their bodies in honor of the idol]. So, the people without understanding [stumble and fall and] come to ruin.

The Message puts the same verses as follows:

They'll eat and be as hungry as ever, have sex and get no satisfaction. They walked out on me, their God, for a life of rutting with whores. "Wine and whiskey leave my people in a stupor. They ask questions of a dead tree, expect answers from a sturdy walking stick. Drunk on sex, they can't find their way home. They've replaced their God with their genitals. They worship on the tops of mountains, make a picnic out of religion. Under the oaks and elms on the hills they stretch out and take it easy. Before you know it, your daughters are whores and the wives of your sons are sleeping around. But I'm not going after your whoring daughters or the adulterous wives of your sons. It's the men who pick up the whores that I'm after, the men who worship at the holy whorehouses—a stupid people, ruined by whores!

Here it is. Hosea begins to speak of a spirit of prostitution. Or if you decide to go with The Message wording, then you would say their genitals are their god. A spirit of prostitution is another pattern we continue to see. A spirit or wind (wind, breath, and spirit are the same word in Hebrew) that is blowing through, turning the attention of men from their wives and from their God to themselves.

In the case of Hosea, these men were turning from God by worshiping other gods which, even if there was no temple prostitute, he "sacrificed" to, any worship of another god is still spiritual idolatry. Then, what's further, as these men visited temple shrines and had sex with these prostitutes, they turned their backs on their wives as well. There are numerous references in both the Old and New Testaments that warn us to flee extra-marital affairs and youthful lusts. Knowing that the men of Israel were willingly jumping in bed with other women is overly concerning. Not only were they worshiping other gods, but they were also committing adultery.

And today, this same wind is pushing men away from God by making porn an idol. They watch and act on themselves in ways that pleasure themselves, but drive them away from their families. How do I know that this spirit of prostitution applies to pornography and not just intercourse? Well, the verse goes on to say that they were led away morally. And any type of sin, in this case, sexual sin, is immoral. What's more, we already know that idolatry has internal roots and motivations that cause an outward action. In the case of Hosea's time, these families weren't trusting and obeying God. Because they had already compromised in that area of their hearts, it led to the action of temple worship. With pornography, a similar root of mistrust can be found. God isn't being trusted or sought to meet the needs; thus, temptation gains traction and compromise happens.

Whenever someone starts discussing anything about spirits, it can cause concern in some, depending on the church traditions they've been involved in. So, let me assure you, by referencing a spirit of prostitution, I'm not suggesting anyone is demon possessed. But we can't ignore that the Bible says a spirit of prostitution was leading people away both morally and spiritually. Throughout the Bible, spirits influencing people is common to see. Unfortunately, we see extremes in this area today. One person or church will think spirits or demons are around every corner so much so that the demon spirits are the reason the alarm clock didn't go off at the right time. Others are completely the opposite and almost ascribe to the belief that the supernatural doesn't really exist.

Whether you find yourself on one end of the spectrum or the other, or hopefully somewhere in between, there are numerous biblical examples that attest to the supernatural role of angels and demons. Their activity hasn't changed, and the angelic and demonic are involved in our day-to-day lives. While the devil may not have given you a flat tire, it is biblically accurate that evil forces could be throwing darts your way

(Ephesians 6:10-16). Now, these darts aren't giving you that flat tire I just mentioned, but more so these darts may be coming in ways like sowing discord in your marriage, or planting tempting thoughts in the head of your spouse.

And it is these darts that lead to them being led away morally and spiritually. James 1:13-15 AMP gives us the breakdown of how sin can lead us astray. It says, "Let no one say when he is tempted, "I am being tempted by God" [for temptation does not originate from God, but from our own flaws]; for God cannot be tempted by [what is] evil, and He Himself tempts no one. But each one is tempted when he is dragged away, enticed and baited [to commit sin] by his own [worldly] desire (lust, passion). Then when the illicit desire has conceived, it gives birth to sin; and when sin has run its course, it gives birth to death." So, this spirit of prostitution leads our husbands away by enticing them and baiting them to sin with their own worldly desires. As we read about idolatry, it has its roots in natural desires. The underlying desire may not be in and of itself sinful, but instead of meeting needs in a God-honoring way, people are being led away to meet needs and wants in whatever fashion they so choose.

Many times, these have grown from natural needs to unnatural ways. Hunger is a natural desire, but when people continue to consume and consume to the point of gluttony, it is unnatural and sinful. Another example of such desires is how God created our bodies to rest. Having a Sabbath's rest was a hallmark of Jewish customs and separated them from other people groups in the area. We still have those same desires to have a day of rest, but instead of working and then resting, we have a culture that wants to rest and be entertained and has become lazy. So, it is with sexuality. There is a desire for sex, which is natural and good inside of a marriage. But when one seeks to fulfill those desires through pornography, it is unnatural.

When someone is led away morally, it doesn't take too long for a spiritual falling away to happen, if they aren't fighting. A spouse may make a poor decision to look at porn and realize that nothing happened to his marriage—no one knew what he had done. He wasn't "zapped" by God, so really, it was no big deal. And because sin can be so enticing and because of the way brains are wired, once you go down that path of sin, it becomes easier and easier to do. This isn't unique to sin, but any action repeatedly done becomes easier and easier to do. So, this compromise keeps happening. And if this person is a Christian, they will feel conviction from the Holy Spirit, but they may not repent or change their thinking. If they aren't fighting against this sin in their lives and just let it grow, they will end up being led far from God—both morally and spiritually, just as Hosea 4:12 mentions.

Unfortunately, there is a great expectation present today. This is when we expect God to do everything, and we do nothing. I've witnessed church services where some Christians seemed little moved by someone saying that Jesus is our over-comer, and I can't help but wonder if that's because they aren't seeing that reality in their life. They are struggling and falling and have hurts and hang-ups that aren't changing. As long as we are alive, we are going to have some type of temptation, but what are we expecting God to do and what are we doing? It seems like many want God to be the great fixer. He fixes the problems while we sit on the couch and change nothing. We must ask ourselves, are we striving to get closer to Him, are we praying much, are we fasting, are we worshiping? Are we seeking to understand what the Bible says about the matter or are we content with living a life of struggle?

Is that how God wants us to live? No! I think not. God loves us more than we know and in ways we don't understand, but just as we have expectations from our children, God does with us as well. I don't want this to become a works-based theology; however, there are some actions that our spouses need to take as believers to ensure that they are being disciplined in trying to have clean minds. Of course, not only does this apply to the struggle with pornography, but it can apply to many things. This is when your husband must decide, is he going to do the hard work and fight to begin to have a disciplined mind? Or is he going to continue a pattern of self-destructive behavior?

Some spouses will immediately make the choice to fight and begin to change. Like Johnnie, they may still compromise from time to time initially, but they are still fighting. They are confessing their sin to God and asking for His help. While Johnnie has made poor decisions and even though those pathways in his brain are still forged and temptations still come, he is doing the best he can to stay close to God and make wise decisions. While the road to mental abstinence may be a long one that has relapses, as long as your spouse is fighting and committed to fighting, then you're headed in the right direction—even if you haven't arrived at the destination yet.

JOHNNIE: You can't do both. You can't be committed to porn and committed to God.

As we continue through this portion of scripture, it states that because the men were engaging with prostitutes, they wouldn't have an increase in their descendants. As you remember, one reason they engaged with temple prostitutes is because they want to be fruitful. And they thought their sexual sacrifice at the temple would help them to that end. However, their families weren't increasing.

In Exodus 23, God told the Israelites that if they served only the Lord and obeyed him, then, among other things, they would have no miscarriages and no barren women among them. Later in Deuteronomy 28:1-9 we see a similar promise. If the Israelites obey the Lord and serve him, they will be blessed. These verses mention the blessings of the Lord in almost every walk of life—your womb, your fields, life stock, and safety from your enemies. But the Israelites didn't uphold their end of the covenant and instead of experiencing those blessings, they were experiencing the opposite. Their descendants weren't increasing, their captivity and deportation to another land was looming, and their families were falling into the same lure of sin. Rather than turning to God, they continued in their sins.

This portion of verses comes to a close by saying their daughters and daughters-in-law were getting ensnared as well. As if to assume that what the father is active in, it can be "passed down" to his children as well. They become affected by his sin or by the same thing that he is. However, it also says God won't punish them. I'm not saying that we get off with a free pass, but I do find it intriguing that it puts the blame of this on the father's head and that it doesn't affect just him, but the other members of his family.

This brings me to another interesting aspect of the porn struggle. This next part may sound odd, but I know it happened and Johnnie would attest to this as well. Johnnie couldn't get away with porn very long before I found out. Sometimes he would choose to tell me without me asking or without him having a reason to tell me. But there were many times, he had a reason to tell me because it was affecting me and the kids in the house. It would happen in various ways, but inevitably, something spiritually rooted would happen. There were times I would have dreams that would lead me to ask Johnnie if he had been looking at porn again. Other times, it wasn't a dream, but rather I would feel extremely uncomfortable and almost scared in my own house. And that's not normal for our house.

As our kids have gotten older, I've noticed that there have been times when they have woken up scared. I would tell Johnnie about these out-of-character things and many times we narrowed it down to two things. 1. He had been looking at images he shouldn't have or 2. Something was watched that shouldn't have been. When I say we watched something we shouldn't have, I don't mean we watched porn together. We are strict with movies, meaning we don't watch rated R movies, and it is seldom we watch PG-13. We are careful about any shows or movies that are shown in our house. However, there have been times in our ignorance we started watching something and turned it off because it wasn't appropriate, or just because we felt that we shouldn't watch it. Interestingly, I have found multiple sources that have linked pornography consumption with demonic oppression.[4, 5] Now, don't freak out, once again I'm not suggesting anyone is demon possessed. Those who are unsaved can be possessed by demons, but those who are saved cannot. However, believers can be oppressed by the enemy. This possible link would explain why the times after Johnnie had an indiscretion, things would feel different.

Theologically, how does all of that work? Honestly, there isn't a clear answer. There are biblical principles that support this idea, but I don't have a chapter and verse to point to that says, "when you watch inappropriate things—whether porn or otherwise—the atmosphere of your home changes." When I would approach Johnnie with these out-of-character things and we narrowed down what happened we concluded that whatever line was crossed must have let something evil in with it. It opened the door for the enemy to attack our family. We can't see how or what comes into our homes spiritually. We know from the Bible that there are supernatural forces at work around us. We know there are angels and demons/evil spirits that can try to influence us. Inevitably, once Johnnie made things right with God, right with me, and we would pray over the house, those feelings would be gone.

While we may not have chapter and verse, as I mentioned, there are principles in the Bible that support this. In James 4:1-10 AMP, we have an interesting passage. Take a moment and read it. I will include verse 7 here just in case you didn't read. Verse 7 says, "So submit to [the authority of] God. Resist the devil [stand firm against him] and he will flee from you." Conversely, this means that when we don't resist, the devil can stay. If we continue down the road of temptation and continue to feed those thoughts and dwell on them, he won't leave. When we read about the temptation of Jesus, we read that after Jesus used the Bible to fight, the devil left for a more opportune time (Luke 4:13). We know from Ephesians 6 that our war is with our spiritual enemy. In Ephesians 4 we read that we are not to give the devil a foothold. Not only those passages, but the aforementioned passage from Hosea 4 also further illustrates that a spirit can impact a family. When there is willing sin, we are opening ourselves up to further temptation. I know we are not the only family who has experienced this. I've heard from others who have experienced the same things, and I've heard parents explain how God would usually communicate with them regarding the sins or dangers of their children.

It's a good reminder that not just with porn, but on a day-to-day basis, what you see affects you. What you willingly see and listen to is what you are allowing in your mind. Our struggle is to be against darkness (Ephesians 6) and when we watch things that promote a will contrary to the Lord, which would be darkness, it affects us. It provides seeds. Just as good seeds produce good fruit, so if we plant a bad seed in our mind, it can produce negative effects. If we are planting seeds of bad language, sexual images, murder, etc. we are in essence putting bad seeds in our minds.

The Bible is noticeably clear about the battle with Satan, demons, and principalities. It's real, it exists, and it's something we have dominion over. Just as we can plant our own seeds by watching and listening to things that promote unrestrained violence, sexual immorality, and bad language, so our enemy can hurl flaming arrows or darts our way (Ephesians 6) to try to tempt us to do anything in word, deed, or thought that is contrary to right living in Christ. It's no wonder we would feel we had opened ourselves up to oppression from the enemy when there had been participation in sin. It's because we have. We've gone down a road that is promoting sin and with each view, each song, and each action we push ourselves further and further away from the holy standard that God demands.

Unfortunately, what is let into your home matters. While some may say it's just pictures or it's just a video, it isn't. They are seeds. Seeds that can affect not only your spouse, but it can affect you and your family. These things become seeds the enemy can prey on to influence you. Some people say, "I can handle it". But should you be able to handle it? Why would you want to? Our maturity in Christ isn't measured by how much inappropriateness we can handle, but rather by how much like Christ we are. Luckily, not all seeds are bad. Your home and your life can be different. We'll cover that in the next chapter.

As we navigate toward the end of this section of Hosea, it ends by saying that "a people without understanding will come to ruin." Without an understanding of what? What is going to keep people from coming to ruin? The Bible doesn't explicitly say what type of understanding the Israelites didn't have. But it can be assumed that it means that people who don't understand God's covenant and the laws and promises associated with it, will come to ruin.

What does that mean for us? The question is, how can we have an understanding so that our spouse, our marriage, and our family doesn't come to ruin? Well, it starts by understanding that this is a two-fold understanding. There's a spiritual understanding and a practical understanding.

Thankfully, we are under a new covenant than what Hosea was under. And because of this new covenant based on better promises (Hebrews 8:6), we can approach God boldly when we are tempted and in need of Him (Hebrews 4:15-16). We can have a personal relationship with God because we are now the temple, and His Spirit resides in us. This spiritual understanding is an understanding in which you and your spouse, learn to fight temptation and walk in the victory that your relationship with Christ provides.

The practical side is where you learn to put barriers and other practical things in place to ensure that your family is protected from pornography and other triggers. And that's where we are heading next, determining how to live your life considering the compromise your spouse has made, as he is hopefully on the road to recovery. We will be talking about how you live this out practically and spiritually. If your spouse isn't interested in stopping and doesn't seem to care about his addiction, keep reading, we'll be covering that soon, too.

Notes:

1. Morris, Robert. The Principle of Purity. YouTube, You-Tube, 8 July 2018, www.youtube.com/watch?v=v61-Oib-ZO4A&list=PLcvtxCTYiflWfS9-BmOUOZmsrBJuCyvD-V&index=2&t=642s.
2. GotQuestions.org. "Why Was the Worship of Baal and Asherah a Constant Struggle for the Is-raelites?" GotQuestions.org, 4 Sept. 2018, www.gotquestions.org/Baal-and-Asherah.html.
3. Meeker, Margaret J. Boys Should Be Boys: 7 Secrets to Raising Healthy Sons. Ballantine Books, 2009.
4. Wayne, Luke, and Matt Slick. "What Kinds of Things Can Open You up to Demonic Oppres-sion?" Christian Apologetics & Research Ministry, 10 Dec. 2020, carm.org/about-demons/what-kinds-of-things-can-open-you-up-to-demonic-oppression/.
5. Stone, Perry F. Purging Your House, Pruning Your Family Tree. Charisma House, 2011.

"Our maturity in Christ isn't measured by how much inappropriateness we can handle, but rather how much like Christ we are."

13.

Accounta-billa-buddies

hen my grandfather returned from the war, things were different. He eventually became a Christian, married my grandmother, and started a family. You would think that after experiencing something so traumatic, yet victorious as war, you would hear about it. But it wasn't the case with him. He barely mentioned it. He kept all his feelings and experiences buried and hardly talked about them. So much so that my grandmother got rid of his uniform because she didn't think it was important to him.

At some point during the 80s, he started going to veteran meetings. He was around other men who experienced the same or similar war stories and that began a change in him. Over time, he began to open up and start discussing his experiences. By the time I was growing up in the late 80s and 90s, I started to hear his stories. Until his death, he told them to anyone who would listen, and he rarely missed a 4th Infantry veteran's meeting.

Why did it take so long for Pap to talk to other people

about his experiences? Well, he never did say exactly why. But, eventually, he was able to move on mentally and, I believe, experience some healing from his experiences. Ultimately, he had a choice, he could keep doing what he was doing—which was ignoring what he was a part of—or he could start doing something different and see a change.

So it is with you. I understand that your marriage isn't going to be as good as new overnight. You aren't going to be over the betrayal and hurt immediately. I understand that this may be a long process for the two of you to work out, and there are no guarantees. But, if you keep doing what you have been doing, the chances of things changing are very small.

You may be wondering what to do now. How do you live each day in light of the compromise made? How do you walk wisely and have an understanding that will propel your husband and family forward during a tumultuous time? I can't tell you how long this season of life will last, so it is important to have a plan in place that will address the spiritual and practical aspects of this struggle. In the last chapter, I briefly mentioned the need to have a spiritual understanding and a practical understanding. Meaning, it is imperative to have a spiritual understanding of how to fight for yourself and your family using scripture. Luckily, there are also practical things that can be done to help spouses as they are (hopefully) pursuing a pure mind, as well as things that can protect your family. Putting these fences in place, while they may not be fun, can give peace of mind and hopefully prevent further compromises from happening.

Accountability

I don't remember what the conversation was about, I

just remember who said it and writing it down. One Wednesday night a few years ago Johnnie's brother-in-law coined, to my knowledge, the phrase "accounta-bila-buddies". It's a much cooler name for an accountability partner. If you have grown up in the church, you are probably familiar with the concept of having an accountability partner and you may even cringe at hearing the phrase. Even though it is a great idea, it hasn't always been practiced well. Because of that, I want to give you a few tips to help ensure that you and your spouse don't fall into the same trap that has caused accountability to perform badly for some.

That being said, accountability is of utmost importance. When we look back at Cain and Abel in Genesis 4, in just a few verses, the boys are born, grow up, offer sacrifices to God, and then one is dead! The story moves pretty fast.

I find two things in this passage intriguing. The first is God's conversation with Cain. Cain offers a sacrifice to God, but God doesn't accept or respect it. We don't have a lot of background on this story, but somehow Cain knew what type of sacrifice he was to bring. I have heard it taught many times that Cain should've brought the first of his fruits from the ground, just as Abel did from his flock. And that could be the case. I've also heard that Abel's offering, the one God accepted, had bloodshed, but Cain's didn't, this argument makes sense as well. However, no one really knows for sure. It amazes me that God comes to Cain and in essence tells him, "Cain, why are you sad that I didn't accept your offering, you know what you are supposed to bring to me." Then comes Genesis 4:7, God says that sin is crouching at Cain's door and its desire is to rule over Cain, but God goes on to tell him that he, Cain, can rule over sin.

Cain had the chance to rule over the sin that was

crouching at his door, should he obey the commands of God. But we know what happened from there. In the very next verse, Cain and Abel were out in the field and Cain killed Abel. Once again, we don't know the details of what happened, we just know that sin ruled over Cain instead of Cain ruling over sin. When God asks Cain about Abel, Cain responds by saying, "Am I my brother's keeper?" Almost as if he is trying to be sarcastic with God. He is trying to tell God that he isn't responsible for his brother. Of course, God knows exactly where Abel was. His blood was crying out from the ground for justice.

Just as sin was crouching at Cain's door trying to rule over him, it is also at our husband's door seeking to do the same. But it does make me wonder, are we to be our husband's keepers? In some regards, no. We are not responsible for their decisions, only they can control that. But it is our responsibility to help. The word "keeper" can alternatively be translated as watchman. Are we supposed to watch out for our husbands? Yes. Are we supposed to support them and help them toward this goal of mental purity? Yes. Thus, accountability comes up.

Accountability is important. Your husband needs to have someone he can go to for the purpose of discussing his problem with porn. It doesn't have to be you. He may feel comfortable talking to you about it; however, he may feel more comfortable talking to another man. The most important thing is that he is talking to someone about the issue. Obviously, this "someone" is in the confines of a mutually spiritually encouraging relationship. Porn accountability is not two guys who might be lying to each other about porn. We've all been there, right? Maybe not with porn, but you may have had an accountability partner when you were younger, and you knew that either yourself or the other person wasn't always honest. That scenario is exactly what we want to avoid. You want your husband to be reaching out to someone trustworthy who will encourage, not beat down, if your husband does slip up. It must be someone he can be honest with.

If you are the person that your husband is accountable to, then take the responsibility seriously. Don't fail to ask him because you are afraid of his answer. I have fallen into this trap many times. I didn't want to know the answer, so instead of asking, I just avoided it. That type of attitude wasn't helpful. Avoidance isn't ideal, but neither is hounding.

You don't want to flip to the other extreme and be constantly asking your husband if he was checking out that girl while the two of you were watching the news. Find the balance between the two and remember that your husband is your spouse, and you are in this together. You aren't fighting against him; you are fighting for him and your family.

Don't be afraid to ask him what the best way to approach the conversation might be. Many times, we get embarrassed asking questions that seem obvious or that may portray us as being uninformed, but to have strong communication you need to ask those questions from time to time. For instance, I asked Johnnie on a few different occasions, "How do you want me to ask? What's the best way to bring up this topic? How often should I ask?" Not only does this confirm to you the best way to approach the matter with your husband, but it also sets the expectation for him that you will be asking.

Additionally, if you are the person your husband goes to when he looks at something he shouldn't, be willing for this to be a joint accounta-bila-buddy relationship for you, too. We mentioned this in an earlier chapter, but it is worth reiterating. Just as you know your husband's weak point, make sure he knows at least one area in your own life you want to improve. This can be a great time for the two of you to keep each other accountable and encourage one another. He is giving you permission to speak into his life about this issue, it is perfectly acceptable to give him the same permission into your life. At the end of the day, you want your relationship to be one where iron is sharpening iron (Proverbs 17:17) and that you are spurring one another on to love and good works (Hebrews 10:24).

One final verse and perspective that speaks to the need for accountability is from the book of James and our pastor when we lived in Alabama, Chris Hodges. At one point Pastor Chris mentioned that confession to God brings repentance and confession to others brings healing. He said this in reference to James 5:16 AMP which says, "Therefore, confess your sins to one another [your false steps, your offenses], and pray for one another, that you may be healed and restored. The heartfelt and persistent prayer of a righteous man (believer) can accomplish much [when put into action and made effective by God—it is dynamic and can have tremendous power]."

While confession can be hard to listen to when the compromise has happened time and time again, it is an important aspect of accountability. If Johnnie never confessed his missteps, there would be a rift between us. I may not know it, but he would. Eventually, it would probably come out. And when it came out, it would have been more egregious because the offenses had spanned a longer period of time. In my opinion, you can't be truly intimate with someone and still have secrets regarding your compromises with porn. I'm not suggesting you must know every aspect of what he is viewing, but there does need to be openness and honesty in your relationship.

Whether your spouse bears his soul to you or whether it

is to another guy, he should talk to you at some point. You need to know how he is doing. This may sound odd but try to set certain goals so when your spouse reaches those benchmarks, you celebrate. These goals will depend on each situation. But perhaps it is to go two weeks without looking at porn. Or perhaps a month. At the end of the two weeks or month or whatever the goal is, do something to celebrate if he was able to stay clean. It's important to celebrate small accomplishments because it builds confidence. There are definitely some spiritual roots to addiction and overcoming addiction, but there are some practical things we can do to help spur us on, too. Creating excitement around him staying clean can be one way to do this. It doesn't have to be anything big or expensive, but it can be something simple that you may not have done otherwise.

HOW IT WORKED FOR US:

We got to a certain point in this journey where the only time Johnnie would slip up would be when I was out of town for multiple days—which didn't happen often. I remember one of the first times when he told me he hadn't "messed up" while I was gone. We were sitting in a restaurant eating burgers and fries and I almost started crying I was so excited. I wanted to shout it to the restaurant what had just happened, but I figured it would be both embarrassing and the other patrons wouldn't care. I told Johnnie, "We have to celebrate!" He told me he didn't want his avoidance of lustful thoughts to be dependent on getting a prize. I understood, but I still wanted to commemorate it. He fought for himself, me, and our family when it would have been easy to sweep it under the rug. For that, he gets celebrated.

14.

Filters

Ignorance can be dangerous. You may think your husband or children are not in danger of wandering online to look at things they shouldn't, and while I hope that is the case, it is not one based on statistical data. Using filters on your devices is not only a practical way to keep your spouse from looking at inappropriate images, but it can also help keep any of your children or teenagers from getting ensnared in the same temptation.

Sometimes, all it takes is someone saying something that can make the biggest impact. For Johnnie, it was Craig Groeschel, pastor of Life.Church. Over the years, we commonly would watch his weekly sermons throughout the week. But the first time we heard him speak was during a First Wednesday service at the Church of the Highlands. During his sermon, he discussed how his smartphone wasn't as free as they are made to be. He went on to explain he has filters on his phone to ensure he doesn't slip up and look at something he shouldn't.

But he's a pastor, you might say! Surely, he doesn't

struggle. Unfortunately, pastors are not immune to this temptation. I would argue that pastors are probably tempted more than what we know, especially considering the impact they make. Pastor Craig is wise to guard his phone. He went on to say that while he may not be struggling at that moment, he might have a moment of weakness in the future and if that moment does happen, he has a physical filter to keep him from doing something he would regret. When Johnnie heard the pastor from the largest church in America say that during a church service being broadcast to over a dozen campuses as well as online—his perspective changed. Johnnie realized that maybe he wasn't a weirdo for struggling with porn and that it is okay to have a practical fence put up for when temptation would come.

Up to that point, we didn't have a filter on any of our devices. I found out later that Johnnie wanted filters, but he was too embarrassed to have them. He didn't want other guys to find out and think he was a freak. He hated to think that someone would need to use his device and then he would have to explain why he has filters on his phone. Additionally, he kept saying he didn't want to be dependent on a filter to keep him from sinning, but he wanted to have the personal discipline and conviction to do it himself. I respect that, and I understand where he is coming from and I agree. I don't want him dependent on a filter when his heart and mind are relatively unchanged.

On this particular Wednesday after Pastor Craig mentioned a private matter such as having a filter on his phone, the crowd applauded him—they didn't gasp in horror. They respected the fact that he was committed to keeping his mind clean and having accountability to his family and church. After that, Johnnie wasn't embarrassed anymore if he had a filter, he just wanted this issue to be fixed.

Instead of looking at having a filter as a point of weakness, he looked at it as a strength because it is so freeing. Yes, his phone is limited in its functionality, but he doesn't have to worry as much. Even when tempting thoughts come into his head, it is easier for him to dismiss them because he knows he can't access anything on his phone. He knows that if he wanted to look at anything, he would have to work at it. He may have to go to the gas station that sells the pornos. It would be something he would have to plan and hide. Even though phone restrictions are a relatively small barrier, it gives him the presence of mind to be able to fight more effectively.

I admire the guts Johnnie had to admit he needed the help, and his willingness to pursue the solution. I can't promise that your spouse will be so willing and ready to jump on board. However, this isn't a topic that you need to wait for him to offer to put on his devices, but something for you to talk about and something for you to strongly encourage. For me, I wish I would have suggested it a lot earlier.

JOHNNIE: Having a filter in place earlier would've kept me from going so far into pornography. It would've changed things.

After hearing Pastor Craig, Johnnie finally got to the point where he said he was ready to take action. He was still going back and either looking at porn or looking at some type of images he shouldn't be viewing that led to sin. While he didn't want to depend on a filter, he also said he needed it. I know a lot of people think about filters and think about how they will get in the way or be limiting. But most of the time, it will not be an issue.

When thoughts like that creep in and tempt you to leave your family unprotected, remember Proverbs 27:12 AMP "A prudent man sees evil and hides himself and avoids it, but the naive [who are easily misled] continue on and are punished [by suffering the consequences of sin]." As wives, potentially as moms, and hopefully as Christians, we need to be prudent and help our families avoid evil. Filters are one of the best ways to do this, from a practical point of view.

While the porn industry is getting bigger and bigger, luckily, so are the options in filters and controls that can help limit explicit content exposure on most devices. Moments of weakness may happen. Your spouse will be tired or hungry or temptation will come when he least expects it. And when those weak times are experienced, it gives peace of mind to have another barrier set up.

You have a lot of choices when researching filters for your devices. An online search for porn filters will return numerous results. There are some techy options that are free, there are paid subscriptions, and apps, which give plenty of options. One such internet filter we have used over the years would email me a list of questionable sights my husband had visited. There are a lot of options out there, and the choice the two of you make will be determined by your needs. Most of these options aim at preventing inappropriate content for your entire family. While the context here is your spouse, you must keep any children in your home in mind as well. It is unwise for you to assume that your children and teenagers don't need some type of filter set up for their devices.

Johnnie was one of those kids they thought would never

be looking at porn. In our experience working with students, many of them have already seen porn by the time they get to high school. The students we worked with were kids who had grown up in church and were not students you would expect to have been tangled up in porn. So, protection for your entire family is a very prudent decision.

Depending on the type of phone you have, you may be able to enable a free filter from the operating system. We have used both Android and iPhone and we have found that iPhones are much easier to utilize parental controls that block inappropriate content than Android devices. It doesn't mean that Andriod devices don't have it, we just had problems finding it in their operating system. When we had Android devices, we had a paid filter subscription with its own web browser that we used.

The way we have Johnnie's iPhone set up is twofold. The first, which can be done for any type of phone or device, is that we enabled Safe Search from the main search engine. Safe Search is "supposed" to block anything inappropriate from search results and even help ensure the image returns are appropriate. You might not think image returns are that big of a deal, but I have searched for something seemingly innocent and after a few lines of images, it became raunchy. Safe Search is not perfect, but it does decrease the number of inappropriate search results.

The second filter we have set up on Johnnie's phone involves the parental controls in the main settings. It feels weird setting parental controls for your husband, but for the time it is a good thing. As we have said throughout this book, we all have imperfections that must be confronted. Unfortunately, this is your husband's and it is neither easy nor convenient to deal with. The parental controls on the iPhone allow you to have a lot of control over what your spouse can do. For instance, if I wanted to disable Johnnie's ability to download apps, I could change that setting. This is important because some apps can be very inappropriate.

The app setting is also important for your kids or teenagers. If you don't know much about some of the popular apps that are being downloaded today, do some research. They aren't all as innocent as playing Oregon Trail. Another setting is related to media content. You can ensure the music and shows he watches don't contain explicit content. Most importantly, you can choose to limit the adult content websites. To take it a step further, you can block certain websites. If you are anything like me, you probably don't know any specific porn websites. That's why I have the adult content blocked. Luckily, Johnnie has been open with me to tell me if there are other sites that aren't porn sites but may have images or content that are tempting for him. For those sites, I just put the website in, and it will block him from accessing it. Don't be surprised if some of the websites seem innocent. Johnnie has told me about certain social media sites that I would consider innocuous, but for him, it is a temptation, so it's blocked.

Just enabling these parental controls has done a lot to help. I've been surprised at the times we have looked something up and he will tell me the page is blocked for him. Most of those times I'm not sure what on the web page has led to it being blocked, but I would rather my husband's eyes be free from temptation. One other big perk of enabling restrictions for the iPhone's web browser is that it disables the incognito window. While incognito windows are great for buying Christmas presents without anyone knowing, they are awful when it comes to porn. Johnnie told me the incognito window or private window was one big tool he would use because he knew the incognito window wouldn't have a tracked history. Since we have enabled the restrictions, he knows he can't use it. SO helpful. He has told me that it is a relief knowing that he doesn't have access to it because it means it isn't even a temptation. The best part of this is that to change any of these settings, you have to create a pin number that only you know. Having this password set up is another level of security so those settings can't be changed without your knowledge.

Unfortunately, when we had Android devices, we weren't able to customize them as much. I'm not saying it can't be done, but we just never found any options within the phone itself. Now, that may have been related to the model of phones we had. Perhaps they have more options now. If you have an Android phone, it's worth your time to look around at the various settings to see what options they may have. Or you may need to do as we did and either use a paid filter or switch to a different type of device.

The aforementioned options are free, which is always a plus. However, there are many other paid filtering options that work across most devices. Nothing will be perfect. Unfortunately, some people will find ways to get around the filters that are in place. But having something in place that will monitor, block, and alert you if porn is viewed is essential. Additionally, ensuring your spouse doesn't have access to a private browsing window or incognito window, whatever your internet browser calls it, is paramount.

At one point during our marriage, Johnnie was a pest control technician. One aspect of his job included going into a house's crawlspace. He saw quite a few snakes under houses in those cramped quarters. Once, we were discussing how and why snakes are in crawlspaces and he mentioned that if they have a food source, usually mice, then a snake will stay under there. One way to get rid of snakes and ensure they don't return is by eliminating their food and water source. While that conversation's intention had nothing to do with porn, I immediately saw a connection.

One way to keep porn out of your home is by eliminating the source. If there are websites that can be accessed, movies that can be watched, or images that can be looked up that will allow your spouse to go down the road to lust and masturbation, it's going to be a long, hard road for him and for you. However, if you can eliminate those triggers by having filters and being careful with what you watch and listen to, then porn won't have much to feed off. Just as a rodent in a crawlspace can help create an ideal environment for a snake to live, so we can allow things in our house that will make the environment susceptible to another compromise. That being said, as a wife, you can do everything possible to create an environment, but your husband must be willing to make a change too.

While we may not have the same temptation as our husbands, we are never above that temptation. While it may not be tempting now, it is better to have something in place to prevent the temptation should it ever arise. Protect your family. It may be inconvenient, it may be another username and password to remember, and it may even be an extra charge every month. But protecting the minds and hearts of our family is vital. It's worth repeating from the last chapter, the mark of godliness isn't how much you or your spouse can handle (content wise), but it's how Christ-like you are. Some may say that it isn't right for a person to have so many restrictions on their phone. However, I say that if it helps my guy become more Christ-like, I'm all for it. Johnnie and I would rather be Christ-like and not be able to handle bad language and inappropriateness, rather than think we can handle it and set ourselves up for a lifetime of struggle.

More Practical Ideas

Accountability and filters are vital in this battle, but there are a few other practical things to keep in mind that need to be covered.

This first one has to do with how you react in the future when/if your husband looks at porn again. I hate to say, "when your husband looks again" and set that type of expectation, but I also want to mention it as a possibility. I want you to expect the best, but I also don't want you to be ignorant of possible slip-ups.

Recently, Johnnie told me the way I would react when he would confess helped him tremendously. He told me he didn't think he would be free today if I hadn't acted in love. Because I tried to always encourage him, I didn't hold it against him, and I didn't bring it back up over and over, he was able to move forward. He went on to tell me that when he would confess, he was opening up to me and fully deserved for me to lash out at him. He said he felt he deserved for me to punish him. Because I chose not to, it helped him be more open in the future. He likened it to handing me a sledgehammer to take all the hits I wanted. But I chose not to. I chose to love him, encourage him, and try to help him find a road forward instead of choosing to damage him. Obviously, he wasn't implying I was physically going to hit him with a sledgehammer, but he did say he felt he deserved punishment.

In light of that, be cognizant of how you react when

your spouse has a moral failing. It does not mean you make light of the situation or treat it as "no big deal", but it does mean you show him love and respect. It means you don't bring it up in a different argument as ammunition. It means once he confesses it, you let it go and choose not to hold it against him. You figure out how the compromise happened, then try to figure out what can be done differently next time. If the indiscretion comes up, or if you have questions about it later, that's fine to address it, but don't keep beating your spouse over the head with the ways he has messed up.

This forthcoming practical example may seem minor, and it may not matter to you, but when Johnnie apologizes, I don't say, "It's okay." It's not okay. His action was not acceptable. Usually, I'll respond by saying, what you did was wrong, and it hurt me. But I forgive you. Let's figure out a way to do things differently next time.

Please, do not hold this struggle over your husband's head. I may sound like a broken record, but the two of you are in this together. Even if he is acting childlike in some ways, don't treat him like a child. Treating him that way can drive him further into porn. Your husband is supposed to be the head of the house, and when you treat him like a child it can cause him to detach and go to porn, because there he feels he has control. That being said, when I say that your spouse is the head, I'm not implying that you are not a leader. I am not trying to imply anything regarding gender equality, but rather going back to the idea that when woman was called a helper in Genesis 2, it wasn't this idea of a subservient, less than equal person. Life without her was not good, she is needed. To put it this way, without woman, man doesn't become what he is supposed to be. Proverbs 18:22 AMP says, "He who finds a [true and faithful] wife finds a good thing and obtains favor and approval from the Lord." So, how you handle this is of utmost importance.

What About Sex?

The last thing I want to cover in this chapter is bedroom activities. Sometimes, the hardest time to have physical intimacy with a spouse is after you know they have compromised sexually. I've heard many wives say that they would not have sex with their husband if they found out he was looking at porn. And I have to disagree here. Why would a woman do this? There are two reasons, 1) The wife just found out and is not emotionally ready, and 2) It is used as a threat to convince their spouse to stop looking. There have been many times I've told Johnnie that it is emotionally, thus physically, hard to connect with him knowing that he didn't have the self-discipline or control to stop what he had done earlier. He was very understanding. He knew it was his fault. So the first reason, I completely understand.

However, withholding sex from your spouse long-term isn't the best way to handle the situation. There is a big difference between withholding yourself because you are emotionally struggling with his addiction and withholding from him as a punishment. I Corinthians 7 discusses some teaching about marriage. Paul instructs the church in Corinth that husbands and wives should share their authority over each of their bodies, and they shouldn't withhold themselves from each other, unless it has been agreed upon for the purposes of prayer. Then, he says, "but come together again so that Satan will not tempt you [to sin] because of your lack of self-control." Obviously, Paul is

185

not dealing with a pornography situation or any type of wrong-doing, but it does show that when couples keep themselves from each other, it does open the door for MORE temptation to come. Refusing our husbands will not help them not look at porn, in fact, it may do the opposite! It may open the door to more temptation and more lies.

One thing I have learned, because Johnnie told me, was that the times I was really hard on him in this struggle were the times he was still tempted and would feel more pressure to hide it from me. I understand the marriage bed is to stay undefiled (Hebrews 13:4). And I know your husband has been deviating from that path. But punishing him by withholding sex is not the way to get the desired change. He is not a child, and you do not want that type of relationship with your spouse. You are setting a dangerous precedent by treating him that way. Remember, this is not a fight of you against him, but rather this is a fight that you fight together, the two of you against the enemy trying to tear your marriage apart.

Maybe your spouse is not willing to change or very slow to change. Perhaps he doesn't see anything wrong with it—what then? If he is callous toward your feelings and emotions, do you have the same approach? That's a great question and we are going to cover all of that in the section about having a spouse that doesn't want to change. Whether you are in that position or not, I would encourage you to not skip over it. It has very important information, no matter what stage of the fight you are in.

Additional Resources

The focus of this book is the spousal side of a porn addiction, so this book probably won't help your husband very much because it wasn't designed for him, it was designed for you—his wife. However, there is a plethora of books, videos, and articles that have been created to help men who are struggling with porn. I would love to recommend some different ones, but a lot of it will depend on your spouse and whether they prefer video or print resources. Either way, there are a lot of resources out there that are designed specifically for men struggling with porn. X3 Watch is a filter that we have primarily used, but they also have had resource articles, videos, and even online small groups at one point to help their users. I know others who have used Covenant Eyes, there are others such as Net Nanny, Net Angel, and more. Please, take some time and figure out a filter that will work for your family's needs, as the few I mentioned are not an all-inclusive list.

There are also resources that aren't specifically for a porn addiction, but rather for addictions or mental hang-ups in general. Books like *The Bondage Breaker* or *A Mind Set Free*. Books such as those can be immensely helpful. Once again, this is a physical issue, but it also has spiritual roots. Attacking this monster from both a practical and spiritual perspective is necessary.

15.
Spiritual Understanding

Every time I think through Pap's stories, I can see them in my mind. I can imagine my grandfather, then 20 years old, landing on Utah Beach, France, not knowing what was going to happen. One thing he did know, his watch no longer worked. While that sounds like an odd realization when you are invading another country, he retold the story many times of how he had a watch that his father, Sam Glenn, had given him. The day the 4th Infantry landed on Utah Beach (about 2 weeks after the initial invasion), he stormed the beach along with his fellow men then he happened to notice that his watch wasn't working. Apparently, after their initial landing, he had time on the beach to try and fix it. And however he tried to fix it, he said the second hand flew off and it was lost in the sand of Utah Beach. Just as a piece of him was forever in that sand, so the events of the war were forever with him.

This battle that you are in with porn is not one that you

will one day forget about, either. It's not something small that will just fade into distant memory, but it will be something you look back on. I pray that you, along with myself, will be looking back at this battle victoriously, just as my grandfather knew his actions in WWII helped to bring peace to a world shaken by war.

Unfortunately, wars aren't always won quickly. Ours is no different. While it may be short-lived for some, more often it is something you have to keep contending for. In a physical battle, there have to be strategic moves to help ensure victory. In the fight we're facing, we must do the same. We have to be strategic and pair both a spiritual understanding and a plan of action with some of the practical ideas we've already discussed.

Hosea 4:14, which we referenced a few chapters ago, says without understanding people will come to ruin. While the Bible doesn't specifically outline what type of understanding that is, I think having a spiritual and practical understanding in your approach to conquering porn is one way to look at that passage in light of our current topic. So, spiritually, what understanding do we need to have? I believe this is twofold as there is a spiritual understanding that we need to grasp, but there are also spiritual steps we need to take from that understanding. We can have all the understanding, but if we don't put it into practice, we aren't acting wisely.

What Do You Believe?

It's important to settle one thing at the beginning of this chapter. I'm assuming you are a Christian. When I say a Christian, I don't mean you just go to church or that your family has a good reputation. I mean that you have a redemptive covenant with Jesus Christ, you've asked him to forgive your sins and save you (Romans 10:9-10). If you aren't a Christian, make that change now. Don't wait. (More information in the back of the book!) God doesn't want you to be powerless or without an advocate. He has a plan and a purpose for your life and the lives of those in your home. Despite popular opinion, a life lived in God's way is more satisfying than doing things the world's way by satisfying every lust you may feel. Knowing Christ as your Savior is the foundation on which everything else is built.

Maybe you have been a Christian for much of your life, or perhaps while reading this book you have realized your need for Christ and have become a Christian. Either way, it is vitally important to understand your relationship with Christ. I'm going to be transparent with you, when I got saved, I got saved mostly because I was so scared of dying and going to Hell. When I made the decision to follow Christ at 9 years old I knew if I died I was going to Hell. Even though I was a good person, and even though I had been at church most opportunities (Sunday morning, Sunday night & Wednesday night), it didn't matter because I hadn't asked Jesus to forgive me.

I was carrying my own sin and I was going to have to pay for it unless I turned to Jesus. At the time, I didn't really care about any other benefit of having a relationship with Jesus other than avoiding Hell! But as I grew older and began to read the Bible, I realized there was a lot more than Hell avoidance. We don't have a relationship with Christ only to get to Heaven, meaning obtaining heaven as our home isn't the sole purpose of being a Christian. We follow Christ and have a relationship with Him for many other things. Likewise, our spiritual lives are important now. In fact, I've heard a pastor say that our relationship with the Lord now will determine how we spend eternity.

Not just where we spend eternity, but the rewards we get when we get there, among other things.

Once you choose Christ, things change. 2 Corinthians 5:17 AMP says, "Therefore if anyone is in Christ [that is, grafted in, joined to Him by faith in Him as Savior], he is a new creature [reborn and renewed by the Holy Spirit]; the old things [the previous moral and spiritual condition] have passed away. Behold, new things have come [because spiritual awakening brings a new life]." We are transferred from the kingdom of darkness to the kingdom of light (Colossians 1:13). Instead of being held captive by sin, we have power over sin. Instead of being hopeless, we are hopeful. We have the Holy Spirit living inside of us to empower us and to guide us. Because of Jesus, we can now pray directly to Father God. Because of Jesus, we have authority over the powers of darkness. All of these benefits have nothing to do with us or things we have done, but rather what Jesus has done.

To summarize, God's covenant with us is based on the blood of Jesus. Because of his sacrifice, we have direct access to God. We know from both the Old and the New Testament that God loves us. He wants us to be joined with him. He doesn't want us to suffer eternal judgment and He isn't in Heaven just waiting for us to make a mistake so He can zap us. No, it's the opposite. He created us for good works that were established before we were born (Eph. 2:10). John 10:10 AMP says, "The thief comes only in order to steal and kill and destroy. I came that they may have and enjoy life, and have it in abundance [to the full, till it overflows]." Life in the Lord is not one of hopelessness, but it is one of confidence. Because Jesus lives within us, we can do mighty things.

Not only is being a Christian important for you

and your family but being a Christian is the only way to be equipped to fight the spiritual nature of a pornography addiction. Why does being a Christian better equip you to fight this fight spiritually? Because you have hope in Christ and His abilities to intervene that unbelievers do not have (Romans 15:13, Psalm 147:11). You have the love of Christ living inside you (1 Peter 4:8, 1 John 4:19). You can forgive because Christ has forgiven you. You can fight this fight in prayer. Lastly, you have the authority to stand up to the attempts of the enemy on your marriage and family. Knowing all of that makes this look like a one-sided fight, doesn't it? When I think about all of that, I think, "This addiction doesn't have a chance!" You have the Lord on your side, you will not fail.

It is here I want to make an important distinction that was mentioned earlier, but it is worth repeating because it can be easily forgotten. When your spouse continually keeps going back to porn—your husband is not the enemy. This fight is not against your husband, this is a fight against evil. This is a fight against the lust of the flesh. (1 John 2:16) It is so easy for you to feel like you are the victim because it seems like he is doing an action of his own will and you are being hurt. You are the victim and he is the perpetrator. And while there is some truth to that statement, I know from my conversations with Johnnie that he felt stuck too. He felt he had no control at times, in essence, he was a victim too. He was looking at things and doing things he knew were wrong but found himself bound by them.

So, when I say the Lord is on your side, I don't mean the Lord is not on your husband's side. The Lord is on his side too, as the Lord is on the side of righteousness and He is against evil. He is against lust. He wants your spouse to be free, too. In Mark 10:8, Jesus quotes a passage from Genesis (we read that a few chapters back) that says when you marry, the two become one flesh. Don't alienate your spouse, help him fight. Whether you like it right now or not, you are one flesh. Our spirits are separate, but you are knit together physically.

Know Your Enemy

Knowing all the power and benefits we have of being a Christian, this seems like a one-sided fight, doesn't it? Like there is no hope for any addiction, right? Well, yes and no. While there is nothing that is stronger than the Lord and nothing can defeat Him, we do have an enemy, Satan, who has set himself up against God. From the very beginning, he wanted the glory that was due to God. Satan wanted people to worship him, not God. When he was kicked out of heaven, he took some of the angels with him as they had fallen into the same deception. Since that time, Satan has been using the same tactics to try to distract worship from God. While I know no one who has an altar in their house set up for Satanic worship, when we are distracted from following God's will and God's way, Satan is winning. When we fight through our own power instead of God's power, we are glorified, not God. And when we take the glory instead of God, Satan is winning. It doesn't have to be an obvious affront to God. Just as having an idol doesn't mean you have a wooden image of another religion in your home.

If you are wondering why we are talking about Satan it is because he is the author of sin. He was the first one to sin. Because of his influence on Eve and Adam, sin entered the world. Perversion and lust come from him. Because he is so crafty and deceptive, it's important we have a spiritual understanding of him. Never do we want to focus on him more than we do Christ or exalt him or give him credit for more than what we do with God. He is not equal with God. However, on this side of Heaven, he is our spiritual adversary, he is the enemy.

The Bible paints a pretty interesting picture of this fallen angel, Lucifer or Satan. From both Genesis and 2 Corinthians we know that he was the one who deceived Eve. And from when sin entered the world until now, it hasn't stopped. In John 8:44 Jesus says that Satan is the father of all lies and half-truths. He wants to deceive. In 2 Corinthians 11:14, Paul says Satan masquerades himself as an angel of light. Meaning, he doesn't look deceptive and evil, in fact, he may actually look the part, but once the mask comes down he has no light in him, for he is the kingdom of darkness (Colossians 1:13, Ephesians 2:2,3). I Peter 5:8-9 says Satan or the Devil prowls around like a roaring lion seeking someone to devour. In Ephesians 6, which is one of the premier chapters regarding spiritual warfare, the Bible says, "For our struggle is not against flesh and blood [contending only with physical opponents], but against the rulers, against the powers, against the world forces of this [present] darkness, against the spiritual forces of wickedness in the heavenly (supernatural) places."

Finally, in the book of Revelation, chapter 12 verse 9 the Bible says, "And the great dragon was thrown down, the age-old serpent who is called the devil and Satan, he who continually deceives and seduces the entire inhabited world; he was thrown down to the earth, and his angels were thrown down with him." Chapter 12 goes on to say that Satan is the accuser of the believing brothers and sisters. He is accusing us before God night and day. In chapter 20 of Revelation, we read of Satan's ultimate final defeat where he is banished to no longer be able to deceive the people of the world.

Pretty grim picture of our enemy, right? He and the powers of darkness will use any tactic possible to try to distract us away from the Lord. Picture it like this: Imagine a time before you and your husband were married, back to when you were engaged. At that point, while you aren't married yet, you are promised to each other. You love each other and are excited about your wedding. Contrary to popular practice now, you want to remain pure until your wedding. It's important to you and it's important to your future spouse because you don't want to be joined with anyone else but your spouse. You have that desire, but there is someone who keeps trying to distract you from your soon-to-be spouse. Maybe they are always trying to interrupt your time together, or they want you to spend time with them alone. It may seem innocent, but it really isn't.

This guy has been around for a while and really, he wants you to commit to him instead of your fiancé. He keeps trying to do things to woo you and pull you away. Ultimately, you have the choice. You can choose to stay committed to your future spouse and keep yourself from anyone else, or you can choose to give in to the curiosity, the excitement, and the attention and join yourself to someone else. Take that same analogy and apply it to your walk with the Lord. He is the husband and we, the church and individually, are the bride. Satan and his forces represent the other person who is trying to keep you from your future spouse. We are the bride of Christ and Satan is trying to do anything in his power to tear us away from the Lord. He doesn't want us to have pure lives, he wants us to be deceived, to have strife, confusion, sin, and addiction. He doesn't want to see us joyful in the Lord or happy in our marriages. He wants to ruin our lives. And how does he do that? Big ways and little ways. But, in the context of this book, porn and lust are two ways that he can use to damage not only your marriage but also your spiritual life.

Would Satan really attack a marriage? Shouldn't the powers of darkness be more interested in trying to get pastors to slip up? Yes, the enemy really does want to attack your marriage. Honestly, it isn't just your marriage, but it is marriage in general. Why? What's the big deal? Of course, Satan would want pastors to fall, no doubt. But just because they are high-profile leaders of the faith, it doesn't mean they are the only targets. Marriages are under attack for a few different reasons. First, marriages are a picture of our relationship with God. The church is the bride and God is the bridegroom. Before the relationship of mother and father came the relationship of a husband and wife, since Adam and Eve were formed, not birthed. This is the longest human relationship that has ever been established. And, when it is biblically based, it is beautiful and life-giving. When marriages fail, a picture of our relationship with God fails. Also, marriages fail because people fail and when people fail, people get hurt. When one marriage fails, it can affect how women view men, men view women, how children view authority, how children are raised, how children view marriage, and finally how children view the opposite sex. Marriages are extremely important.

Another reason why marriages are under attack is the fruit of marriage, children. In Joel and later in Acts, there is a prophecy about the last days stating there will be an outpouring upon all flesh, and one age group it targets is "sons and daughters". Ironically, Americans are having fewer babies than ever, which has interesting implications looking toward the future.[1]

Taking the focus off America as a whole, look at the religious implications. Christians are not the population having the most children. In fact, I heard a recent video of an Islamic man telling a reporter that Sharia law would become reality because Muslims are the people group/religion that are having the most children.[2] He plainly said that other populations aren't having as many kids. I'm not advocating for us to have tons of children for discipleship and evangelistic purposes; however, it does shed a very interesting light on the importance of raising children in a healthy, Christian home.

I admit, this is a bit of a rabbit trail, but if we aren't raising our children in a healthy, Christian home, they may be more likely to fall away and not follow Christ. As a Christian, I believe the only way to Heaven is through Jesus (John 14:6) . I don't want anyone to die without Jesus. With that knowledge, raising a family who will continue to be devoted followers of Christ is one of my most important jobs as a mom.

Knowing that information—rabbit trail included—it is easy to see why marriages are under attack. If the marriage falls apart, it can have a ripple effect throughout the family whose impact can negatively affect that generation. Whether by way of pornography, sexual immorality in other ways, unnatural desires, financial strain, or communication issues, it's clear to see that marriages are under attack.

Now, you're reading this book because your spouse has an issue with porn, so the fact that your marriage is under attack may not surprise you. And if you are anything like me, when I found out my husband was looking at porn, it really affected me, too. Not only was the enemy getting my husband to sin, but I didn't feel confident in myself. I was upset, and there were times I really didn't want to forgive him. I had so many opportunities to sin during this process. Thankfully, because my spiritual understanding was on a good foundation and growing,

I had a firm footing to face this without sinning. I wasn't always perfect but considering all the different footholds I could have allowed; I came out victorious.

Not only in fighting for your spouse, but also for your own sake it is important to understand the spiritual enemy. While this has not been an exhaustive exposé on Satan and demons, it is enough to give you an understanding. But thanks be to God that we are not powerless against this force. Rather we have authority.

Prayer

Why does this matter? Why lay that foundation? In an earlier chapter, I mentioned the need to know who you are in Christ, and this is a great time to bring that up again. Knowing who you are and your position in Christ is so important. When you have the spiritual understanding of who our spiritual enemy is and the understanding of what our covenant with God empowers us to do, it can change our understanding of prayer thus, how we fight for ourselves, our spouse, and our families. It will allow us, as women, to arm ourselves, in essence. When we arm ourselves with the knowledge of who God is and what He has empowered us to do, we cannot be defeated. Romans 8:37 says we are more than conquerors through Christ! Not weak, powerless defeated people!

This is where theology meets action. It's one thing to know God and to know we have access to God, but it's another thing to put our knowledge into action in the form of prayer. Praying for your spouse is something you can't go without doing. Don't put the book down, even if you feel discouraged thinking about prayer. I know sometimes it can be hard to pray. However, I also know that there are times when prayer comes so easily. I heard a quote years ago that said, "You have to get a taste of it to get a taste for it." Meaning, the more you pray and experience the presence of God, the more you realize how much you need to experience His presence. There are days when praying for 10 minutes may seem hard. But don't give up! Keep pressing in and you will experience those times of prayer when you dread having to stop.

Unfortunately, I think many people think that prayer is something they can do without. They think it is something that won't really work. I have a few ideas of where they get this idea, but it mostly comes from how they understand their relationship with God. If they think they are powerless and they are just subject to whatever happens and are just waiting to get to Heaven to experience Jesus, then yes, it would seem pointless to pray. Others would just rather talk to their friends or hear feedback from their social media accounts than take their burdens to the Lord. And I understand—I really do. When I talk to my friends, I get instant feedback that usually makes me feel better. There is a certain satisfaction in getting to talk to someone else about what is going on in my life. Don't get me wrong, there is a time and place for talking with someone close to you about what's going on in your life. However, where we have gone wrong is when that is our first and only outlet. We think that talking about it in that atmosphere, maybe even getting Godly advice and encouragement, is a replacement for prayer. It isn't.

One resource that has changed my prayer life is a prayer guide that our former church in Alabama, Church of the Highlands, supplies. I've listed the link in the footnotes.[3] The aforementioned resource is a great place to start if you need a resource to help you have a prayer plan. That being said, how do you pray about a porn addiction? First, there are your personal feelings and healing to consider. Then, there is the obvious need for your husband to be free from a porn addiction. Both of those things need to be vocalized in prayer.

Yourself

Let's start with you. How do you need to pray for yourself during this time? The answer to this question is going to depend largely on how you are feeling. If you are struggling with forgiving your spouse, that should be your first prayer stop. Remember, Matthew 6:14 AMP says, "For if you forgive others their trespasses [their reckless and willful sins], your heavenly Father will also forgive you." Ask God to help you forgive him. When you are praying, remember you are talking to God as your father who is in Heaven. Meaning that you can be honest with Him. He knows how you are feeling, so it does no good to lie. I know the feelings of betrayal and hopelessness and despair. You feel let down and lied to. In my times of prayer, God heard about those feelings. He knew how frustrated I was that Johnnie kept relapsing. He knew how sad I was.

When you are praying for yourself, ask God to heal your heart, to renew your love for your husband, to give you understanding, and to give you wisdom. Wisdom is promised to you if you ask the Lord for it, according to James 1:5. Each situation is different, and will need the wisdom that comes only from the Lord in knowing how to approach this issue. I know the only reason I was able to handle some of Johnnie's confessions was because I continued to strive to keep my relationship with the Lord strong, vibrant, and growing. I know this changed how I handled these situations because so many times I had the peace of God when I really expected to have the opposite.

In discussing peace, if you need a verse to keep at the forefront of your mind, I would suggest Philippians 4:7 AMP, "And the peace of God [that peace which reassures the heart, that peace] which transcends all understanding, [that peace which] stands guard over your hearts and your minds in Christ Jesus [is yours]." I love this verse because it mentions the peace that stands guard over your heart. The peace of God can act as a guard. When unexpected circumstances or confessions bombard you, you can have the peace of God. God doesn't start working once the unexpected happens, He is already at work within you. You can have the peace of God before the situation ever comes before you. In my experience, I had the peace of God, but then I felt bad that I wasn't emotional. I know, that sounds weird. But it wasn't that I had grown callous to Johnnie's confessions, but rather I had the peace of God guarding my heart. This empowered me to respond to Johnnie in the most Christ-like manner possible, instead of reacting emotionally and saying things I would regret.

Your Spouse

Once again, your husband is not your enemy! Have I mentioned that yet? When you are praying for your husband, you aren't praying hell fire and brimstone down on him, no matter how upset you may be. Rather you need to be praying for him to be encouraged.

JOHNNIE: It can be a discouraging battle when you feel like you can't stop looking at porn, you feel trapped.

Pray that your spouse feels the encouragement and hope that only the Lord can give and that he can overcome this struggle. Pray that your spouse will have the discipline to say no to temptation. I'm hoping that your spouse is a Christian, but if he isn't, pray that he will become one. Your prayers can include one that is rebuking the enemy from this situation. We know this issue has spiritual roots, so attacking the spiritual root of the issue, which is the enemy who is trying to get your spouse to commit a sin, is necessary!

You don't have to use this prayer, but if you need some guidance, here's a way to start. Over the years as I have prayed for Johnnie, it has sounded something like this:

God, I thank you for Johnnie. I know you love him, and you know I love him. God, I'm frustrated, sad, and I am ready to see things change. God, I know you know what is going on, but I am asking you to intervene. Father, please encourage Johnnie and give him the discipline to say no when the opportunity for porn presents itself. God may our house be a place of your presence and of your light. Father, in the name of Jesus I bind the spirit of lust that is coming against my family. I know it isn't from you, therefore it is not welcome nor allowed in this house. Father may you guard our minds and our hearts. Father give us wisdom on how to fight this battle. We are declaring victory in the name of Jesus.

As you are praying for yourself and your husband, remember, you have the Lord on your side. I John 5:14-15 AMP says, "This is the [remarkable degree of] confidence which we [as believers are entitled to] have before Him: that if we ask anything according to His will, [that is, consistent with His plan and purpose] He hears us. And if we know [for a fact, as indeed we do] that He hears and listens to us in whatever we ask, we [also] know [with settled and absolute knowledge] that we have [granted to us] the requests which we have asked from Him." God doesn't want your spouse to continue in sin, so you don't have to wonder if it is God's will for him to be free from this addiction, so pray confidently knowing the Lord hears you!

Being rid of porn is a big struggle for your spouse, but it can also be a big struggle for you, if you let it. You might be tempted to lash out at him after he has made another mistake. You may struggle with those feelings of self-doubt and self-worth. There may be times when you ask yourself if you really do want to be married to this man for the rest of your life. Doubts may come, temptation may come, and defeats may come. But you must remain vigilant, hopeful, and never give up.

If you were to ask me the one thing that has helped me personally as we've gone through this, I would tell you—every time—that my relationship with God has been what has made the difference. Not talking with friends, not crying myself to sleep, but those times of prayer and resting in the presence of God. In those times I would feel encouragement and hope invade even the deepest places of hopelessness. Don't skip prayer. Run to prayer. If you don't have a good routine of praying, start now!

More important than prayer length is prayer consistency. If I pray an hour once a week that's nice. But if I spend a few minutes every day putting God first, it will make all the difference. You will find that what may start as just a few minutes of prayer starts to go longer. Or you may find that throughout the day you begin to pray while doing the small things. I think that is the spirit behind the verse in 1 Thessalonians 5:17 ESV which says, "Pray without ceasing."

Throughout the last few chapters, and broadly throughout this book, I've presented the case for both the physical and spiritual roots of this addiction. Because of this, it requires a combination of practical physical barriers as well as a spiritual understanding to fight this in prayer. But, what if he doesn't want to change? Well, it's time to tackle this hurdle. While I can't guarantee a change in him, this next chapter will equip you with ideas of what to do if you find yourself in that situation.

Notes:

1. https://www.nytimes.com/2018/07/05/upshot/americans-are-having-fewer-babies-they-told-us-why.html
2. https://www.youtube.com/watch?v=jWT9zhKcuJo#action=share
3. https://assets.highlands.io/21days/2022/pray-first-guide.pdf

16.
Great Expectations... Or Deflating Hopes

I wish I could say that every husband would be changed in an instant. They looked at porn once, confessed it to God and you, then never looked again. Unfortunately, that rarely happens. Some spouses are wanting to change but really struggle. Others may not worry about changing, thinking it isn't a big deal. They may be hostile toward you and your feelings. What then, just give up? It can be easy to have grace for someone who is trying to get things right, but a different story when they are indifferent to your feelings. It can be very hurtful, but don't let that change your attitude toward having forgiveness. We forgive no matter what. However, the addiction is still hurtful. There isn't a way to be immune to hurt and pain; however, that does not mean you give up and file for divorce.

I took some time to talk with my father-in-law, who,

aside from pastoring a church for many years and being a missionary for many years, also practices in marriage and family counseling. We talked at length about how to conduct yourself in a marriage when your spouse is resistant to change. We discussed questions like, do you still have sex during the addiction? Should you go to counseling? How do you find peace in the midst of the turmoil? Let's talk about these because they all relate.

1. We're never having sex AGAIN!

Okay, that may be a little extreme. We discussed this earlier regarding having a spouse who is willing and wanting to change, but change is slow. Taking it a step further, what do you do when your spouse is acting in a way that is completely hostile toward you and the situation? Obviously, I want to tread very carefully because each situation is different. First, I want to echo what I said in a previous chapter and what my father-in-law confirmed too, withholding sex doesn't stop the addiction to pornography. What my father-in-law also said, which I had never thought about from this perspective, but continuing to have sex within a marriage reinforces where sex is appropriate. In the bounds of the marriage bed, assuming both are consenting, it is acceptable, but outside of those bounds it is inappropriate and it is sin, whether it is physical or digital.

Knowing that sex is important to marriage, and it keeps a marriage strong, how do you do that when you are constantly at each other and there is no peace between the two of you? We all know that when you are arguing and upset at each other, sex is not the first thing on your mind. And if that pattern of emotional hurt continues, the attitude of hostility toward each other and to sex will continue as well. That's why there needs to be some honest communication and a plan to move forward. Sex is not a bargaining chip; it is an essential part of marriage. Knowing that withholding yourself can drive your spouse further into his addiction, there needs to be a path back to a reconciliation point where you would be willing to have relations with your spouse again and start building your marriage back up. At the end of the day, the goal is a restored marriage, not a bitter divorce.

I want to remind you again, you were married for a reason. While that reason may seem a million miles away right now, your spouse is still your partner. There may be a lot of hurt feelings and betrayal between you right now, but don't lose hope.

What can honest communication look like? Here's an example:

"I know we haven't been with each other lately. I'm very hurt and I feel like you don't care. I don't want to continue like this, so can we figure out a way to move forward?"

At this point, your spouse may have some ideas, but he may not. You ignoring his addiction and acting like it doesn't exist is not a way to move forward. Depending on how the conversation goes, it may be an appropriate time to bring up counseling. Which is what we are discussing next.

2. Counseling

I'm so glad that God has gifted men and women counselors, like my in-laws, in helping marriages be restored. Practically speaking, if your husband is resistant to change, he may not be on board with putting filters on his devices. Additionally, he may not want any type of accountability. What then? There comes a time when you need to consider marriage counseling. Whether your spouse wants to change or not, if you get to the point where it seems like you are not moving forward, or perhaps your spouse is completely against changing, then consider counseling.

I know some people refuse to go to counseling because they don't like how it may "appear" to others. Well, that's a bunch of bologna. May we never get so proud that we put our appearances before our most important earthly relationship. Here's the thing, the same people who may not like the way that therapy appears to others, are going to be the same people who won't like the "appearance" of a divorce, either. Their appearance and other pride-related issues may keep your spouse from being willing to pursue the counseling route. However, I've come to notice that when it comes to therapy, people around you are generally a lot more supportive than you would imagine.

If your spouse is hostile toward you, counseling would be an appropriate step. I think some spouses are hesitant to go to counseling over matters like this because they feel like they are going to get ganged up on. Think about it, if you were the offender and you knew the main reason you were bringing a third person into the mix is because of your actions, you might feel a bit intimidated. Once again, let's be honest with each other. If your spouse falls into that category, try to ease his mind.

Let's be clear, even though he got himself into this, it is still hard on him on some level. Feeling like he is the "bad guy" may not spur him on to wanting to change. I would encourage you to approach this situation so your husband is clear that you are both trying to find a way forward. This isn't a session to just complain about him. Counseling is a place for the two of you to find a way forward. I can say from experience that you probably haven't handled his addiction in the best way possible either. So, there may be things said about how you have handled the situation that have hurt him that need to be dealt with, as well. While Johnnie and I didn't have to go to counseling for this issue, there were times I handled the situation wrongly and I did hurt him, and those were things we had to work through as well.

With all the different stories I've heard from women dealing with this, I've heard so many different scenarios and personalities. Counseling has done wonders for some, but others are hesitant to begin because their spouse has a "silver tongue" and is great at telling people what they want to hear, without actually having to change. Just remember, you have a voice. If you are in counseling and your spouse is just saying things that sound good, be honest about it in a respectful way. Counseling can be a long road. Dr. Ramos, my father-in-law, reminded me that short-term therapy doesn't really work. Getting out of a porn addiction is a lifestyle change and it takes time to build foundations that help down the road. It takes time. Don't give up!

If you decide to pursue counseling, but you really aren't sure where to start, check with a church in your community. If you are a member of a church, you could also see what types of resources are available for church members. There may be a member of the staff that would offer counseling to church members. If not, they should be able to furnish some local counselors for you to contact. If you don't want to use a church, you can also check your local health department for a list of counselors or an internet search will give you names to check out.

If your husband doesn't want to go to counseling or to speak with a pastor, consider going by yourself. While you aren't the one with the addiction, there are still plenty of emotional things the counselor can help with. Also, he or she may be able to give you advice regarding your specific circumstance.

How do you talk to your spouse about going to counseling? Here's an example:

"We've reached a point where I want to move forward, but I don't know how to do that since porn is still an issue. At what point would you consider counseling?"

Depending on how the conversation goes, you can then figure out the next steps. Just because he is unwilling to go, it doesn't mean that you don't have actionable steps you can take.

3. Finding Peace

As I see people around me struggling, I look back at what Johnnie and I have gone through and found myself thinking, how did we make it? One realization I keep coming to is that we were able to find peace in the midst of the turmoil. Even though I knew what he was doing, we were able to, in a sense, compartmentalize that part of our lives. We were able to set it aside and realize that while it is an important aspect of our marriage, it isn't the only aspect. We figured out how to get back to our basics—the things that brought us together in the first place—so we could find some peace and try to be reconciled to each other and move forward, even if he was still struggling. One way we did this was to remember and find new common ground.

Porn can really divide a marriage. Try to do things you know you enjoy doing together and see if you can find something new that will join you together. Perhaps it is bike riding, going to a museum, or building something. Find something you both enjoy doing and spend some time doing an activity that joins you together, not pulls you apart. When you begin to focus on common interests and build new interests together, it is giving the back seat to pornography and making sure it doesn't dominate the relationship.

I've been there, sometimes it feels like the addiction might be the only thing you're thinking about. In seeing how other couples are dealing with this struggle, I have found myself thinking: "If you could just get to the point where you enjoy spending time together again, you could get some perspective and be able to attack this obstacle and see it defeated." Even as we are post-addiction, Johnnie and I may be arguing about something and I'm just trying to figure out a way we can end the argument so we can get back to how things usually are between us—joyful and full of life. While it isn't healthy to ignore conflict, there comes a time to look past all the chaos and find a way to reconnect even when you may be unsure of the future.

Back to the Spiritual...

I want to switch gears. In case you have noticed, the pattern that has emerged throughout this book of switching from the practical application to the spiritual application and back again. I firmly believe those two work hand in hand. So, to the spiritual side we go.

Investing your time by spending it with God. In a world of things happening quickly, and exuberant entertainment at our fingertips, it's not surprising that we have lost some of our perseverance. We may pray a few times, but it can be hard to continue in the face of adversity. But remember, just as we said previously, the battle isn't against flesh and blood, or your husband. We need to strive to get closer to God, and that can be done by praying, reading the Bible, fasting, and worshiping. There are many things we can do on a daily basis that draw us close to God. Petitioning the Lord for a change in our spouse, as well as taking practical steps to see that change are important actions for wives to be taking.

The first thing I want to discuss is your words. Be incredibly careful of the things you say. I'm not saying you ignore reality and act like nothing is wrong but do be careful of how you speak about your spouse. Your words have power. In Proverbs 18:20-21 AMP the Bible says, "A man's stomach will be satisfied with the fruit of his mouth; He will be satisfied with the consequence of his words. Death and life are in the power of the tongue, and those who love it and indulge it will eat its fruit and bear the consequences of their words." What you can take from that, is don't go around telling your spouse he can't change or is never going to change. Speak positively and be encouraging. It doesn't mean you ignore reality, as I said, but it does mean that you don't forget the reality of God's Word, either. We can't get so focused on what we see in our husbands that we forget that God can deliver and that your spouse can grow in self-control.

But, when things aren't getting better, how do you react? Chances are that the compromise will happen again. It is certainly my story. It's frustrating, isn't it? When you see the person you love choosing to view porn instead of calling you or contacting someone else to help overcome their temptation. The feelings of hopelessness aren't lost on me. I have experienced them more times than I would like to. And each time I try to calculate my response, it gets tougher. On one hand, I want to be corrective and go through a checklist of things that should have been done. The other part of me wants to keep my mouth shut and not say anything that is going further upset him because he is already feeling bad. So, what do I do? I pray first. I know prayer seems like it is one of the most cliché of Christian disciplines, which is a shame because it is vitally important. Prayer is not inaction and it is not powerless. We know that, "the effectual fervent prayer of a righteous man has great power." (James 5:16)

If you remember, when Johnnie would slip up, he said he felt blind to how I would feel. It was like my feelings were downplayed and seemed very minor to him at the time. Normally my husband cares a great deal about my feelings. He was blinded. We know the enemy can blind the minds of unbelievers from seeing the truth (2 Cor. 4:4), and I think that while your husband may be a Christian, I think he can still be blinded to his sin and the effects of his sin. I would start by praying that the Father would bind the spirit that is blinding your spouse. And that his heart would be softened. If your spouse does not want to change and is indifferent to your feelings, then there is a lot of selfishness and hardheartedness going on in him. And more than likely, there is something else going on. There is nothing you can physically do that is going to change him. For instance, it doesn't matter how you look or what you do for him that is going to change him. What will change him is the Lord and you walking out your faith on a day-to-day basis. While the Lord does the changing, it is us who petitions in prayer for this change, and your spouse making the decision to change.

With a husband who is resistant to change, please don't give up praying for him. However, it does mean that you need to be praying slightly different for your husband. Instead of focusing on self-control to stay away, you also need to be praying that he is sensitive to your feelings and that his eyes would be open to how dangerous and hurtful this behavior is. Pray that he will have a desire to change! Never underestimate how powerful prayer can be. This is why I wanted to lay the spiritual foundation earlier. We can pray boldly, confidently, and with hope and expectation when we understand our spiritual enemy and the authority that we have in Jesus Christ. When we understand that we can stand on the promises of God and claim them for our family, we can have confidence that will not be shaken no matter what the circumstances.

For as long as I have known Johnnie, having a pornography addiction was never something he wanted. He knew it was wrong. But I feel like it took a while for him to realize his triggers and realize that he really could get free. There was also a point he had to get to where he was desperate for change. This desperation didn't come about because of my threats, but rather God working in Him.

I was out of town and he made another compromise. As usual, he told me about it. He then told me he was so mad at himself. He had gone the longest he had ever gone without slipping up and in a moment of weakness, he compromised. His words to me were,

I wanted to throw up.

He was so mad and frustrated with himself that he wanted to throw up. I was upset too, because he had gone a long time—months in fact— and I wanted to ask all these questions like—why didn't you just walk away? Why didn't you call me?! And there is definitely a time and place for those questions, but to see him so dissatisfied with the decision he made, I felt, was a win. Not because I want him miserable, but he must be desperate for change. And to see him be at that point is incredibly positive. Writing this book has been a long process that has spanned years, so it is interesting to see how Johnnie has changed throughout this time. He isn't addicted anymore. And he communicates with me if he's being tempted. It took him a long time to change. Many people would wonder if he really wanted to change because there were times when there was little to no change for a long period of time. But change happened. We didn't give up.

Discouragement

I can be overly optimistic. Being optimistic is a great perspective to have. However, when things don't meet expectations, that sense of hopefulness can be deflating. And discouragement can take over. This book is written from the perspective of having a spouse who wants to change, but he is still struggling and struggling. The process took years, many years. Yet, during that time Johnnie maintained the position that he wanted to change, and he knew that his porn addiction was wrong.

Society today seems to tell us that at the first sign of trouble, we need to jump ship. The message is sent that marriage isn't worth working through. Well, is it? Why do some say that it is? What has happened along the way that made them think it isn't worth it? If it isn't worth working for, then something along the way has been lost. I guarantee you that when you look back on the day you recited your vows to each other, you believed that marriage was going to be worth fighting for. Yet, as time has gone by and compromises happened, you've lost the belief that it can be full of life again. Marriages go through seasons, there may be times when it feels like it is the fight of your life, then other seasons are times of relaxation and ease. Don't get caught in the delusion that fighting hard for your marriage now means that you will be fighting hard for your marriage your entire life. This season will change. There will be times of refreshing.

Discouragement can be so prevalent throughout this struggle. I think it is a rare husband that has an addiction and can stop cold turkey without ever having a relapse. It can happen by the power of God, but most cases do not have that narrative. At some point, many points maybe, you will find yourself wondering if your spouse can change and if they really want or will change. It seems like having a clean husband is a far-off possibility. I found myself discouraged on many occasions by Johnnie's repeated compromise.

We don't have to be dominated by discouragement, though. As I've said before, having a greater understanding of what is going on can help us fight the right fight. What does it mean to be discouraged? Well, if we break down the word, we see two words: the prefix dis- and the root word is courage. Anytime you see the prefix dis- it means to do the opposite of, or to deprive of or just simply, not. Merriam-Webster defines courage as the mental or moral strength to venture, persevere, and withstand danger, fear, or difficulty.

When we find ourselves dis-couraged, that is what is going on. We are lacking the mental or moral strength to venture, persevere and withstand danger, fear, or difficulty. In fact, if you reference that same dictionary, you read that discouragement is defined as depriving of courage or confidence. I've been there! That perfectly describes some of the emotions I've experienced! But discouragement doesn't have to be a part of your daily life. You must know how to fight against it. And where's the best place to look for insight on how to handle discouragement? The Bible.

There were many people who were discouraged, and many great men of God went through some serious bouts of discouragement. One, in particular, I want to highlight is David. If you haven't read some of the stories from David's life, you're missing some amazing stories! This, however, isn't one of those amazing stories, initially. In 1 Samuel we read much of David and King Saul not getting along. King Saul repeatedly tries to kill David and David repeatedly honors and even spares King Saul's life, as he is the King.

Feeling like Saul will never stop pursuing him, David moves to the boundaries of the Philistines. There, the Philistine king allows David and 600 of his men to live. During a military raid, a leader convinced the Philistine king that David shouldn't be helping them, seeing as how they were attacking King Saul of Israel. David and his men returned to their home in Ziklag only to find that their homes had been raided and set on fire in their absence. Their wives, children, and belongings had all been carried off by a different enemy, the Amalekites, including David's two wives (Side note: David may have done it, but polygamy has never been God-ordained).

What now? These men were faced with a devastating

blow, David especially. Not only did he lose his family, but he was the one responsible for all of this. And his men blamed him. They were crushed. They wept until they could weep no more, 1 Samuel 30:4. At this point, the men wanted to stone David. David, distressed and discouraged as he was, "encouraged and strengthened himself in the Lord His God." (v 6) After that, he inquired of the Lord's will in the matter, received an answer from the Lord, then led the charge to get their families back. In the end, all the men had their wives, sons, daughters, and belongings restored to them. Not one thing had been lost or killed. Isn't that amazing? And doesn't that give us a wonderful plan on how to attack discouragement in the face of tragedy?

This is what we can learn from this story. When the unexpected happens, for our purposes here, your husband won't stop looking at porn, it can be devastating and discouraging and sad. Your marriage has been attacked and you feel like you may lose everything. If there was a time to panic, now would be it! But that's not what the Bible says. Instead, at the height of the problem, encourage and strengthen yourself in the Lord. Then, seek His will and watch what God can do to restore and reconcile your marriage. To revisit the foundation I laid earlier in the book, this is why it is so important to have a relationship with the Lord where you are reading your Bible, praying, and worshiping God daily.

To encourage yourself in the Lord, you must know the Lord. To know the Lord, you must communicate with Him. If you are wondering what David did to encourage himself in the Lord, look no further than the book of Psalms. While we don't have a recorded Psalms for this instance in Ziklag, we do have plenty of examples of David singing these songs to the Lord, reminding himself of who the Lord has been and about the steadfastness of His character. David finished the Psalms by praising the Lord and seeing a turnaround in the situation. So, knowing that about David, I have no doubt this is what he did in this situation. We can do the same. We can encourage ourselves in the Lord by singing and praising and worshiping the Lord. Take time in your discouragement to remind yourself who the Lord is. He is not some weak God; He is the Lord God Almighty. He can do anything. His character is unmatched, and he is undefeated. The Lord is our rock, and we can depend on Him.

After David did this, he sought the will of the Lord so he could fulfill it. When you feel overcome by discouragement, take time to figure out the will of the Lord. Now, obviously, you are discouraged that your husband isn't changing. But is that the will of the Lord? Do you really believe that God's best for your spouse is for them to remain unchanged and to destroy your family? I sure don't! I believe that it is God's will for us to walk in victory and have a peaceful, life-giving marriage. To walk out God's will in your marriage, you are going to keep doing the things that you know to do. You are going to keep forgiving, keep loving, and keep serving your spouse and your family. You are going to live out what the Bible says a Christian is supposed to do. That is part of the will of God. Then you are going to keep doing the practical things, along with the spiritual things to take all the steps necessary to see your husband set free. Now, does it take his will, too? Yes, it does. But until his will comes around, you can walk steadfastly in the face of discouragement.

Additionally, just as David sought the will of the Lord and then led the charge to rescue their families who were held captive, you never know what ideas the Lord may give you. Perhaps, He may give you a better strategy on how to help your husband. Or maybe the Lord gives you the exact words to say to help bring reconciliation to the situation. That is the wonderful thing about having a relationship with the Lord. He knows each of our spouses better than we do. And He loves our spouses more than we do. He absolutely wants the best for them, the best for you, and the best for your marriage. I have no doubts that as you pray and seek the Lord, He will show you the way to approach the situation.

The Last Story

The first time I read Isaiah 50, I was on my first foreign missions trip in Panama. We were presenting an evangelistic drama, then at the end, someone would give their testimony and give an opportunity for people to be saved. This particular year, I was really disappointed with my role in the drama. I had one of the most boring parts. It seemed so pointless. My role was a mime. The mimes in this drama were used to create background props. I was a door. Nothing screams, "Come to Jesus!" like being a door. I was hoping to be preaching the gospel to those who need it, instead, I was standing for twenty minutes with my arms up, posing as a DOOR!

I'm not sure if it was our first day ministering or not. But either way, one day I was particularly disappointed with my role. I got back on the bus for a few moments and opened to Isaiah 50. I read verse 7 which says, "Because the Sovereign Lord helps me, I will not be disgraced. Therefore, I have set my face like a stone, determined to do his will. And I know that I will not be put to shame." From there, I had a mission. I too was going to set my face like a stone (flint, in some versions) determined to do His will. So, instead of just being a door, and just listening to the drama unfold around me, I picked a woman out of the crowd and began to pray for her as I was posing as the door. Throughout the entire drama, I prayed that she would come to know the Lord and I prayed that God would give me an opportunity to speak with her about Jesus. This day we were at a school, so the focus was on the kids, but I couldn't quit praying for this teacher.

As the drama concluded and we began to mingle, I tried to find this teacher I was interceding for. But I couldn't find her. We went from classroom to classroom talking to kids, when finally, the teacher I had been praying for came in the room to talk to the other teacher that was in the room! I approached her with a translator and began to ask her about her salvation. She was already saved, but the other teacher she was standing with was not saved and I got a chance to lead her to the Lord.

I share that story and that verse, Isaiah 50:7 to conclude this book. It goes so well with David's story, prior. Even in the thick of this battle, don't lose sight of God's plan and His will. There may be some days that are hard to take. It may be the 3rd day in a row your husband has compromised. You may feel like you're at the end of the rope but take a moment and stop. Encourage yourself in the Lord and let him strengthen you. Figure out what His will is in the matter and seek further guidance if more practical steps need to be taken. Then stand up on your feet, knowing the Word of God, and set your face like a stone, determined to do His will.

How to Become a Christian

If you do not have a relationship with the Lord, now is the time to change that. Salvation is not complicated. Romans 10:9 sums it up: "If you openly declare that Jesus is Lord and believe in your heart that God raised him from the dead, you will be saved."

That's it. There is no special prayer, however, I will provide a sample prayer below. Know this, God loved you so much that He sent Jesus to the Earth to live and die so you wouldn't have to die for your sins. He took the penalty so you could be made right with God. In the words of our former pastor, God doesn't send people to Hell, Hell is a place people go to pay for their own sins. Don't do that. Trust in Jesus today. Don't wait. You will not regret it. Please let us know if you prayed to receive Jesus while reading this book, and we can send you some information to help you in your new life of faith.

Dear Lord Jesus, come into my heart. Forgive me of my sin. Set me free. Jesus, thank you that you died for me. I believe that God raised You from the dead. Fill me with the Holy Spirit, the peace of God, and the joy of the Lord. Give me a passion to reach the lost, a hunger for the things of God, and a holy boldness to preach the Gospel of Jesus Christ. I'm saved. I'm born-again. I'm forgiven and I'm on my way to Heaven because I have Jesus in my heart. Thank You, Jesus!

Want more content?

@JOHNNIEANDASHLEYRAMOS

@RAMOSMINISTRIES

RAMOS MINISTRIES